MOTHER TERESA

The fruit of silence is
Prayer,

the fruit of prayer is
Faith,

the fruit of faith is
Love,

the fruit of love is
Service,

the fruit of service is
Peace.

Mother Teresa

MOTHER TERESA

BY

ELAINE MURRAY STONE

PAULIST PRESS
NEW YORK / MAHWAH, N.J.

Cover art and interior illustrations by Patrick Kelley

Cover design by Cheryl Nathan

LIBRARY OF CONGRESS CATALOGING-IN-PUBLICATION DATA

Stone, Elaine Murray, 1922 –
    Mother Teresa / by Elaine Murray Stone
        p. cm.
    Includes bibliographical references.
    Summary: Describes the life of the nun who founded the Missionaries of Charity, gained wide recognition for her humanitarian efforts in Calcutta and elsewhere, and was awarded the Nobel Peace Prize in 1979.
    ISBN 0-8091-6651-8 (alk. paper)
    1. Teresa, Mother, 1910-   –Juvenile literature. 2. Nuns–India–Biography–Juvenile literature. 3. Missionaries of Charity –Juvenile literature.
[1. Teresa, Mother, 1910-   . 2. Missionaries. 3. Nuns. 4. Missionaries of Charity. 5. Women–Biography. 6. Nobel Prizes–Biography.] I. Title.
BX4406.5.Z8S77   1999
271'.97–dc21
[b]   98–32042
                                                               CIP
                                                               AC

Published by Paulist Press
997 Macarthur Boulevard
Mahwah, New Jersey 07430

www.paulistpress.com

Printed and bound in the
United States of America

CONTENTS

v

FOREWORD

Mother Teresa was a woman of great holiness, humility, and humor. Dr. Stone's book does much to lead her readers to come to know the Mother Teresa of these qualities: a holiness that was rooted in joy, a humility that was rooted in an openness to all God asked of her, and a humor that never allowed her to take herself too seriously.

This book leads us through the journey of Mother Teresa's life, where the dream of the child to be a missionary ("to help people and bring them Christ's love") unfolds into "the pencil in God's hand" that comes to write God's loving signature on the minds and hearts of millions throughout much of the twentieth century.

A young girl, Agnes, in her home church in Albania, prayed one night: "Lord, show me the way." This prayer opened her heart to the journey of a lifetime—a journey that we readers, in a sense, travel as well when we read the pages of this book. This prayer also led her to see, in the life of St. Thérèse of Lisieux, a model for herself, for she too wished to "do ordinary things with extraordinary love." And so she chose the name Teresa.

In the pages that follow we read of a Mother Teresa who drew everyone she knew into the experience of caring for the "poorest of the poor." Her invitation is no less compelling now than it was when she was alive. For the thousands who have followed her example throughout the past several decades, young and old alike, there are memories that will last a lifetime and experiences of God's love in the service of others that will long continue. Do not be surprised if the spirit of Mother Teresa captures a bit of your heart as you read about her, for surely God works through her now as much as ever. One can still hear her saying, when asked about herself or her work: "Come—come and see." And then she would introduce you to her treasures—the poor she loved so much, and the Christ she found in them. Read—read and see.

—FATHER MICHAEL MANNION
Former Chaplain of The Catholic University
Washington, D.C.

CHAPTER ONE

THE CALL

A Happy Childhood

Agnes skipped along the cobblestoned streets. Her feet sent up little whirls of dust into the hot summer air of Skopje. The young girl was on the way to her Sodality of Mary meeting. Although Agnes lived in a modern brick home, many of the houses in this Muslim city were made of mud and stucco. A menacing Turkish fortress loomed on a hill above the city. Men in pantaloons wearing red fezzes passed Agnes in the street; veiled women slithered by.

Skopje was a city of 25,000 in southern Yugoslavia. For centuries it had been a part of the Ottoman Empire. The city was filled with mosques, slender minarets, and bazaars selling Oriental rugs.

The Turks permitted religious freedom for the few Catholics and Orthodox Christians in the area, but churches were required to be small and low. No steeple was allowed to compete with the forest of slender minarets.

Agnes Gonxha Bojaxhiu was born August 26, 1910, when Skopje was part of Macedonia, under Turkish domination. After World War I, Macedonia became a province of the newly formed Yugoslavia. Today it is within the borders of Macedonia.

Her Father's Death

Agnes' parents, Drana and Nicola, were of Albanian descent and devout Catholics. Agnes had a sister, Agatha, and a brother, Lazarus. The entire family attended daily mass at nearby Sacred Heart Church. Nicola Bojaxhiu was a contractor who made a fine living building houses and businesses. He even constructed the town's major theater. When Agnes was nine, Nicola fell sick and died, leaving his wife to support their three young children. What could Drana do? Her entire life had been spent at home taking care of her house and children. All Albanian women were taught to embroider, but Drana's embroidery was considered the finest among her circle of friends. That would be her new career. Drana started by making and selling fine embroidered blouses, scarves and pillows. Her business grew so fast, she had to hire friends and neighbors to help. Soon Drana was running a factory of embroidery. As a result her children were able to continue their education and live as well as they did before their father died.

Missionaries in India

On this Wednesday evening, Agnes arrived at her weekly sodality meeting. She joined the group of pre-teen girls as they filed into the church for prayers. Later a letter was read from a local priest who had left for the mission field in India. Agnes listened intently. She had learned a little about India at the Government School that she and her sister attended. She knew India was in Asia on an immense sub-continent. And she knew that India was also very poor, a place where millions of people lived in squalor and most had never heard of Jesus. Each week the missionary's letter added more to her sparse knowledge. The priest wrote of his experiences in Bengal and of the poverty and suffering of its millions. He wrote about the cruel caste system, with its untouchables who were only allowed to work as collectors of garbage and human waste. After that day's letter was read, Agnes turned to her closest friend to whisper, "Mary, wouldn't it be wonderful to be a missionary? I want to help people and bring them Christ's love." Mary replied, "Why not help the poor right here or convert our Muslim neighbors?"

Show Me the Way

But that was not what Agnes dreamed of doing. When the meeting was over, she slipped into the church to pray alone. "Lord, show me the way," she begged, knowing in her heart that He would lead her in the right direction.

Mother Teresa 1910-1997

Drana had often told Agnes when she needed help, "Child, put your hand in the hand of Jesus. Walk all the way with Him." As Agnes rose from the hard floor, she held out her hand, as though reaching for the certain touch of the Lord. She knew that Jesus would show her the way—when it was time.

Agnes never lost her dream of becoming a missionary to the poor of India. Six years passed before an opportunity came along. It was 1928, the year Agnes turned eighteen. She had just graduated from high school when the Jesuit priest returned to Skopje. He told her the Missionary Sisters of Loreto were looking for young women with vocations to teach in their schools. They especially needed postulants willing to go to India. Agnes could hardly believe her good fortune!

A Dream Comes True

Fearing her family might object, she shared her dream with her mother and Agatha and Lazarus. Drana Bojaxhiu wasn't a bit surprised. Agnes had always been the most devout of her children, often dropping hints of her desire to be a missionary sister. Drana gave her heartfelt approval. "Agnes, this is what you have prayed for all these years," she said. "If Jesus is calling you to this work, then everything will turn out all right."

In May, a letter arrived at the Bojaxhiu's house giving Agnes instructions for her long journey. The Order's Mother House was in Ireland. She was to go there first for her initial training and instruction in English. Then she would leave for India to begin her Novitiate. Later she would teach at the Order's schools throughout that immense country.

The Sisters of Loreto

The Institute of the Blessed Virgin, popularly known as the Sisters of Loreto, was founded in 1609. Mother Mary Ward started a convent in Rathfarnham, a suburb of Dublin. The Sisters' rule was based on the rules followed by the Jesuits. And just like the Jesuits, their main function was teaching.

Ultimately, the Institute spread all over the world. The Irish sisters ran schools in India, and because English was the cultural and business language of India, Agnes would have to learn English immediately.

Off to Ireland

On September 26, 1928, carrying only a small cardboard suitcase, Agnes boarded a train for Paris. Her mother and brother saw her off at the station, and while her mother wept, Lazar taunted his sister, asking, "Agnes, why are you throwing your life away like this?"

Agnes beamed with joy and expectation as she scolded her brother: "You think it is so important to serve in the army of the king of Yugoslavia. I will be serving the King of the whole world." Then Agnes kissed her mother's tear-stained face and found her seat in the coach that would take her across Europe.

Arriving in Ireland by steamer, Agnes was met at the pier by two Loreto Sisters. Agnes looked around in awe.

Everything in Ireland was totally strange and amazing—Ireland appeared so green, not brown and dusty like Skopje. In Ireland everyone was a Christian, and almost everyone was Catholic. Dublin was dotted with magnificent churches with towering steeples. Cheerful bells tolled the Angelus, and priests and nuns in black dotted the clean, wide streets.

At Loreto

As the sisters drove through the iron gates into the convent's property, Agnes noted the great stone buildings and beautifully manicured lawns. Inside, sisters in their black habits moved silently through the halls. Everything was spotless—the marble floors and mahogany furniture shone. But poor Agnes had no one to talk to. Not a nun in the place could speak Albanian or Serbian and Agnes had to communicate with signs and gestures. Obviously she would have to learn English in a hurry.

Agnes only stayed at the Mother House in Dublin for six weeks, which was the length of her postulancy. Postulancy is the time for testing a woman's vocation. If Agnes passed that test, then she faced an even longer sea voyage to India.

Her seven-week ocean voyage took Agnes down the Mediterranean Sea, through the Suez Canal, and around Arabia to Bombay on the Arabian Sea. Agnes did not travel alone but with other young novices, accompanied by an older nun returning to India. They were all dressed alike in long black dresses and black shoes. Bombay was exciting. A bustling city of contrasts, it was the seat of the British ruling class and the home of great palaces of Indian Rajas. Massive government buildings loomed above the streets, yet amid all this display of wealth and power were the millions of poor, struggling to stay alive.

There was so much to learn and see, but the novices were not to stay long. Ahead was the arduous trip by rail across the entire country to Calcutta. When they arrived in Darjeeling, they would begin their novitiate.

The Train to Darjeeling

As the train left the station on the final leg of their trip, Sister Ruth, their chaperone, explained, "Darjeeling is nothing like Bombay or Calcutta. It is a resort city, far from the heat and humidity you have experienced so far. It is in the foothills of the Himalayas, the world's highest mountains. Our convent is at an elevation of 7,000 feet! The air is so clean and pure, that many wealthy Indians and English families come here on their holidays."

One of the novices interrupted, "Will we see snow?" Sister Ruth explained, "Although Darjeeling is only two hundred miles from Mount Everest, the climate is mild. There are beautiful trees and flowers, but none of the tropical heat. Look out the window. Do you see how already the vegetation is changing? And ahead are the beautiful mountains." The train, with its steam engine puffing and straining, went around and around working its way higher and higher above the lowland. The girls saw a vast tea plantation stretching out on both sides. Darjeeling tea, considered the world's finest, was the leading product of the area.

The Loreto Sisters had chosen Darjeeling for their school and Mother House because of its wonderful climate. Many wealthy young ladies, both Indian and English, came here to be educated. The convent was large and impressive. There were playing fields as far as the eye could see, and students in trim uniforms strolling about were proud to be associated with this magnificent convent.

A New Name

A few days after arriving, Agnes was given the habit of a novice. Her dark hair was shorn, and she had taken a new name. She chose "Teresa" for the popular young Saint Thérèse of Lisieux, who was known as the "saint of the little way." In later years when she was known as Mother Teresa she explained, "I chose Thérèse as my namesake because she did ordinary things with extraordinary love." Agnes was now Sister Teresa and she faced two grueling years of the novitiate.

Most of the Novices were Indian girls of the upper classes who had attended one of the Loreto schools. There were eight million Catholics in India but the majority of the population was either Hindu or Muslim. As a matter of fact, India was a vast mission field of 800 million unbaptized natives.

The Loreto Sisters of Ireland specialized in teaching. For three years Sister Teresa studied Hindi and Bengali, the major native languages of India. She was immersed in learning the rules of her strict order, which required many hours of prayer and silence. Later Mother Teresa would reflect on the importance of "silence" for spiritual growth. "We all must take the time to be silent and contemplate, especially those who live in big cities where everything moves so fast. I always begin my prayer in silence, for it is in the silence of the heart that God speaks."

First Vows

On May 24, 1931, Sister Teresa took her first vows as a Sister of Loreto. She was twenty-one years old and fully prepared to launch into a career of teaching. This young nun was eager to "go out and give the life of Christ to the people" as a good missionary. She was sent to the teeming city of Calcutta, hot, crowded, and ripe for the plucking. But the reality of life in Calcutta would be hidden from her for many more years. She was not there to bring the Gospel to the poor, as she had dreamed of so long ago in Skopje. Her destiny was to teach wealthy young ladies in fine schools behind protective walls. Robed in the long, flowing habit of that time, Sister Teresa was assigned to teach history, geography and catechism at St. Mary's High School in the Entally district of Calcutta. She remained there for the next seventeen years.

A part of those years, 1939–1945, brought many wartime hardships. India played a major role in World War II, assisting the Allies against Germany and Japan.

But war brought food shortages. One time when there was nothing to feed the students, Sister Teresa bravely went to the authorities and asked for rice for the school. In 1945 she was promoted to the position of principal of St. Mary's. It was then she began to be called "Mother Teresa." But the privations of the war years, and overwork, brought on the horrors of tuberculosis for Sister Teresa. Calcutta was hot and humid and with its overcrowded condition many Indians carried the disease.

A Call Within a Call

Each year the Sisters returned to the Mother House in Darjeeling for their annual retreat, and so Sister Teresa accompanied them there so that she could recover in the clean, pure air of the mountains.

Sick and weak in September, 1946, en route to Darjeeling, Sister Teresa's life changed forever. As the narrow-gauged train rattled upward toward the snowy Himalayas, the future saint felt a calling—a calling so strong and powerful it could not be ignored. Sister Teresa felt a calling to live among India's poor. Later in her life she said, "I felt that God wanted more from me. He wanted me to be poor *with* the poor and love Him in the disguise of the poorest of the poor." This she named her "call within a call."

For twenty years she had enjoyed a privileged life behind the high walls of her convent school. The Sisters and students ate well and the buildings were clean and comfortable. But many times Teresa felt the despair in her heart for the millions of poor on the other side of the wall. Most had no bed, no home, and no place to sleep, except right on the sidewalk. They lived in the streets and were forced to scrounge in garbage heaps for their food. All were pitifully thin, with pinched faces and arms like broomsticks.

Today, the Missionaries of Charity (which Mother Teresa founded) commemorate September 10 as the day Mother Teresa received her call and began their Order.

Outside the Wall

Sometimes Sister Teresa took her most devoted students outside the walls of St. Mary's to bring food to soup kitchens or medicine to dying babies. The contrast between their lifestyles struck students most profoundly. When any sisters or students fell ill, they were sent to the infirmary and comfortably tucked in under starched white sheets. The patients of St. Mary's received loving care and medication. But the sick and poor of Calcutta lay on the cluttered and dirty ground until death claimed them. Lepers begged in doorways, holding up stumps of rotted fingers, and newborn infants were left to die in garbage dumps. Sister Teresa wanted to do something—anything—to help alleviate their misery.

But as a nun she had taken a vow of obedience and everything she did must be under the jurisdiction and with the approval of her superiors and clergy. To leave her community and live among the poor required a drastic change. How would she go about it?

Into the Slums

She soon found a way to begin. As the leader of the pupils who belonged to a service organization called the Daughters of St. Anne, Sister Teresa collected bandages and simple medicines, such as aspirin and iodine. She led the girls into the nearby slum known as Moti Jheel where they worked to help the sick and injured. But each time was a terrible shock for these young impressionable girls.

Some of the girls nearly fainted from the frightful stench of human and animal waste. They choked on the putrid smoke of poor families cooking over dried cow dung. The sights, smells and sounds were overwhelming to these young ladies, but the courage of Sister Teresa inspired them to press on. They might not have felt Moti Jheel was the proper place for them to be, but for Sister Teresa, this was where she belonged. She saw the face of Jesus in all those suffering, brown faces. She remained focused, for she knew that she must live among them to truly serve them.

Sometimes God speaks to us in our hearts. Be silent and listen carefully, for God may be calling you to a new life of service.

CHAPTER TWO

MISSIONARIES OF CHARITY

A Big Change

Sister Teresa had lived and worked with the Sisters of Loreto for twenty years. She loved them and her students, but God had called her to a new vocation. It would be much more difficult, but its many hardships would draw her still closer to Jesus. Sister Teresa told her superior, "I want to leave the Order and live among the poor." Mother Cenacle was disappointed at losing such an excellent teacher and principal, but she understood. She told Sister Teresa, "You need permission from Rome to be released from your vows." When Mother Gertrude, the General Superior of the Order, found out that Teresa felt it was time to leave, she wrote her, "Getting permission from Rome will take time. But I give you permission with all my heart."

And there were still more hurdles to leap. First, Mother Teresa requested an appointment with Julien Perier, the Archbishop of Calcutta. It was 1948, a difficult time in

India's history, and the vast country was in utter turmoil. For two centuries it had been under British rule, and for decades Indians had been demanding the chance to govern themselves.

A New India

Mahatma Gandhi led the movement for independence. He believed in and practiced passive resistance, and to demonstrate this, Gandhi went on long fasts. Many times he fasted almost to the point of death to make his convictions known about achieving independence for his people. He also led them on a long protest march to the sea, called the Salt March. Finally in 1947, England granted India independence. But still there was no peace. Muslims and Hindus fought each other for dominance. Millions of innocent people were killed in the fighting.

Finally a solution was recommended. India would be divided into two countries. One part was India, for Hindus. The other was Pakistan, for Muslims. People began a massive move to the country of their religion.

But as people traveled from one area to the other, thousands were massacred on the way. To compound the tragedy, Mahatma Gandhi was shot by an assassin of his own faith. In the middle of all this unrest, Sister Teresa called on the archbishop. He had already heard about the Sister at Entally (the area of Calcutta where St. Mary's High School was located) and rumors had reached him of her strange ideas. He knew that she wished to be released from her vows and that she wanted to live among the poor. The prelate wondered if God had a hand in all this. If so, he wondered, how should he settle the situation?

A New Beginning

The archbishop listened attentively as the little nun outlined her plans to live among the poorest of the poor and serve them. He asked her, "Where will you stay? Who will support your work?" "God will provide," she replied. Sister Teresa's simple, direct manner and ready answers convinced the archbishop of her sincerity. God had His hand in her request, he felt, but Archbishop Perier asked Sister Teresa to wait one full year. He also told her to get permission from the Vatican, and, in addition, he told her that a constitution for her new community had to be drawn up. Ten sisters must join her before the constitution would be confirmed, and then the new congregation would be under his authority. In addition to the three usual religious vows, poverty, chastity and obedience, Mother Teresa added a fourth: "wholehearted free service to the poorest of the poor."

In February, 1948, permission finally arrived from Rome for Sister Teresa to leave the Sisters of Loreto. For the first time in her thirty-eight years, the tiny woman from Yugoslavia was on her own. As Agnes Bojaxhiu, she had grown up in comfortable circumstances surrounded by a loving family. Over the following twenty years she had lived as Sister Teresa in clean, beautiful convents and schools. But her position in life and the high walls of her convent had separated her from the realities of India. Now Sister Teresa had permission to share the misery of the poor. And as the courageous little nun walked fearlessly into an unknown future, her destiny was that she would become the most beloved and revered woman in the world.

The First Sisters

Mother Teresa's greatest desire was to bring Christ's love to the poor. Because the word "charity" means love and because she had always dreamed of being a missionary, Mother Teresa put the two together and named her new community, The Missionaries of Charity. Her sisters would support her in spreading God's love to *all* people

The idealistic nun took off the black veil and habit worn by the Sisters of Loreto and in its place she adopted the simple sari worn by most Indian women. Hers was of cheap white cotton with a blue border which she wound around her body like a Roman toga, and clasped with a crucifix at the left shoulder. Because most of the poor had no shoes, Mother Teresa and her Sisters wore sandals. Indoors they went barefoot. They would live as simply as possible; her Sisters would own nothing. Living like the poor with no money, they were to sleep on the bare floor.

Mother Teresa Studies Nursing

But first Mother Teresa needed to learn how to care for the sick. All of her past training had been as a teacher, so Mother Teresa took a train two hundred and forty miles to Patna, in order to study with the American Medical Missionary Sisters at Holy Family Hospital. For four months she took intensive nursing courses. She learned how to dress wounds, particularly the dreadful sores and stumps of lepers. She practiced giving shots to prevent diseases like diphtheria and cholera and she heard lectures on the latest techniques of medical hygiene. She learned everything from how to make the dying more comfortable to delivering a baby. Mother Teresa described her plans to live a life of total simplicity to the hospital's superior, Mother Dengel. She said, "My Sisters and I will eat only salted rice, like the poor." Mother Dengel was shocked and shook her head, saying sorrowfully, "Such a diet will leave your Sisters as weak as their patients. You must feed your Sisters well; otherwise they will get sick and die. All of you must stay strong in order to be of help to others."

Mother Teresa agreed to this principle. Women in her Order would live simply in every way, but substantial and balanced meals would be a must.

Moti Jheel

After taking the train back to Calcutta, Mother Teresa began her work in the slums. She slept in a small room at the convent of the Little Sisters of the Poor. Just before the end of 1948, she started a tiny class in an open space under a tree located in one of the worst slums, Moti Jheel. Mother Teresa had no chairs, books or blackboard for her class. The five ragged children who showed up sat on the ground. None of them could read or write. Mother Teresa began her work by teaching them the Bengali alphabet. Always resourceful, she scratched the letters in the dirt with a stick.

That first year, more children came. Some of her former high school students offered to help. Their parents donated money, paper, and pencils. Some of the girls brought soap. The poor children had never seen soap before and tried to eat it. Mother Teresa patiently helped them to wash in a nearby water tank.

On rainy days, it was impossible to teach in such an unprotected area, open to the elements. Mother Teresa prayed for a dry site, a place with doors and windows. In answer to her prayers the parish priest at Park Circus donated 100 rupees toward her work. With this money, Mother Teresa rented two rooms, one for a classroom, the other to be a set up as a dispensary. Soon there were twenty-one eager students.

Mother Teresa's priest, Father Henry, had a wealthy friend, Michael Gomez, who was a devout Catholic. Mr. Gomez's mother had recently died and his two brothers had moved to Pakistan. Father Henry spoke to Michael Gomez about Mother Teresa and her work. "The entire second floor of my house is now empty," Mr. Gomez said. "The little nun can have it—rent free."

The First Convent

Mother Teresa was delighted. At first she moved into just one room at 14 Creek Lane. It had a chair, a box for a desk and a picture of the Virgin Mary on the wall. At bedtime, Mother Teresa unrolled a mat on the floor to sleep on. This was all that she needed. At this time Mother Teresa also changed her citizenship. It was important to her to be fully Indian like her students and Sisters.

The First Sisters

In March, 1949, the first postulant arrived to join the new institute. She was Subhashini Das, a young Bengali girl. She had been a student of Mother Teresa's at St. Mary's High School, and as a member of the Daughters of St. Anne, Subhashini had carried food to the poor in Moti Jheel.

One unforgettable day, Subhashini knocked at the door. Mother Teresa's heart beat faster as she opened it and heard the young girl say "Mother, I have come to join you." Mother Teresa hugged the girl, then asked, "Are you able to give up everything?" Subhashini assured the nun, "Yes. I know it will be hard, but I am ready." Subhashini took the name Sister Agnes in honor of Mother Teresa's baptismal name.

Now there were two sharing the life of poverty and compassion. When asked in later years why she required her Sisters to live in poverty, Mother Teresa replied, "How can you truly know the poor unless you live like them? Poverty gives us freedom. It means we have fewer obstacles to God." The Sisters' closets weren't jammed with name-brand clothes; they didn't even have closets. Each new Sister received three saris—one to wear, a second to wash, and a third to dry. They were rich in this respect, for the poor owned only the rags they had on. Mother Teresa said of her Sisters' way of life, "Without our suffering, our work is just social service." In the early years, the two Sisters prayed together, rising at 4:30 A.M. and attending Mass at a nearby church. Each day they walked to the slums carrying donated food for the starving and medicines for the sick.

The Order Grows

During that year, ten of her former students asked to join Mother Teresa's Order. Most of them came from middle-class families with servants and many had never even had to clean their rooms. Now, they willingly became servants to the poorest of the poor. They washed the sick who were covered with filth and running sores and fed them by hand if needed. Soon Mother Teresa asked to use other rooms on the second floor. There was more work to do and there were more people to serve. Some postulants had to sleep on the veranda. "Pray while working," Mother Teresa would say. "Do it for Jesus. See Jesus in everyone you help."

The Constitutions

In the Constitutions for her order, Mother Teresa outlined four conditions for entering the Missionaries of Charity: (1) Postulants must be at least seventeen years old. (2) They must be healthy in mind and body. (3) They must have the ability to learn. (4) Postulants must have common sense and a cheerful disposition.

The applicants were given ample time to discover if the life was too hard. Mother Teresa required that a girl spend six months working with the poor before entering the Order. It was important to see first-hand what this life was like. If the sights and smells did not repel a young woman, but rather compelled her to alleviate the misery of the poor, then she was accepted as an aspirant. After the novitiate each girl was instructed to return home for a month to contrast the two lives. If the Order was still her desire, she was professed.

Love and Sacrifice

An important point taught by Mother Teresa was this: "It is not how much you do, but how much love you put into doing it that is important."

At St. Mary's she had taught her students that the poor must be helped through sacrificial giving. "Give up a meal, an outing, a moving picture," Mother Teresa urged. "Your gifts should be offered out of personal sacrifice."

Already trained to sacrifice, the Sisters didn't find their new lives a hardship—quite the contrary, in fact. Simplicity, combined with selfless giving, brought them joy. Most nuns, such as the Ladies of Loreto, rarely left the protective walls of their convents. But Mother Teresa wanted her Sisters to have freedom of movement. If the need arose, they should be able to go into the worst slums at any hour. She made one stipulation: Sisters must always work and travel by twos. This would help them to protect each other.

Problems and Solutions

Naturally, Mother Teresa faced many conflicts along her new path. First, the archbishop had made her wait a year before starting her sisterhood, and, in addition, the Vatican was apprehensive about the entire concept. Rome was already concerned about the many small, new Orders struggling to grow and pay their way, and here was a woman wanting to add one more tiny, obscure group. Besides, it competed with the Daughters of St. Anne in Calcutta who were already doing similar work for the poor in the slums.

Nevertheless on October 7, 1950, Pope Pius XII finally sent his approval of the new Congregation. The constitution was accepted and the blue-bordered white sari became their signature. Most young girls joining the Order had worn the traditional sari all their lives, but they were accustomed to colorful silk saris, soft beds and servants. Now they wore cheap cotton and slept on the floor. Mother Teresa urged them to practice these three virtues: total surrender, trust, and cheerfulness.

But the hard life of the Missionaries of Charity never kept anyone away. Once her Sisters began serving the poor, they rarely turned back. Mother Teresa's work had begun with teaching poor, ragged boys and girls to read. Now it seemed that a new direction must be added as well.

Hell on Earth

Anger and hate grew between Muslims and Hindus in their newly divided country. Millions of refugees moved from one area to the other. Religious persecution had placed their families in danger. Poor Hindus from East Pakistan fled by the thousands to safety in Calcutta. But Calcutta was already crowded with ugly slums.

The over-populated city bulged with masses of poor refugees who had nowhere to sleep. There had never been enough jobs in India before the partition, and now finding work was hopeless. Men and women were willing to work for any scrap of food. Every night hundreds of people died of starvation. Bodies lay rotting in the streets. Over one million people slept, cooked and defecated on the sidewalks of Calcutta. The lucky ones lived in tin-roofed crates or cardboard boxes.

The Dying Woman

One day Mother Teresa was walking through one of the worst slums when she stumbled over a body on the sidewalk. Was it a man or woman? she wondered. Dead or alive? Suddenly the bundle of rags moved. Mother Teresa bent over the still form. It was a woman. The stench almost made her faint. Then she discovered rats and maggots had eaten the woman's feet. The compassionate nun's heart was broken. Mother Teresa asked the people standing nearby, "Do you know this woman?" They all shook their heads. Then tiny Mother Teresa picked up the woman and carried the lifeless form into the receiving area of Campbell Hospital. "Excuse me. Can someone help?" she asked. "This woman is near death." Mother Teresa held up the limp body. The admitting nurse held her nose and answered. "I'm sorry. We can't admit her. She won't live but a few hours."

Mother Teresa didn't budge. The nurse waved toward the street. "It would be best to put her back where you found her. There's nothing we can do here."

Mother Teresa still refused to leave. She stood there holding the lifeless form. Finally it was obvious that the European woman in the blue and white sari would not give in: The nurse grimaced, "All right, put her on this cot. I'll see what can be done."

Help for the Sick Poor

Knowing the dying woman would be cared for, Mother Teresa left and marched straight to the city hall. She asked to see Dr. Ahmed, the health administrator. "Good afternoon, Madam," he said, rising to greet the European woman. Mother Teresa didn't waste a moment. She told him, "No one wants to take care of the sick poor. They are dying in our streets." The doctor nodded. Everyone was aware of the problem.

Mother Teresa continued, "If you can find us a place, my Sisters and I will care for them at no cost to the city."

The administrator's face lit up. "I will certainly look into it." He had heard of the sister's wonderful work in the Moti Jheel. Here was something worth considering.

How was Mother Teresa able to get what she needed

to help the poor? It was her total faith that God would take care of the problem. But *she* took the first step to make it possible. Daydreaming and wishing won't get people what they need. But *doing* something about it will.

CHAPTER THREE

SOME PLACE BEAUTIFUL TO DIE

Kalighat

The next day, Dr. Ahmed, chief health official of Calcutta, showed up to talk to Mother Teresa. Dr. Ahmed informed the delighted Sister, "I have found a place for you." He hesitated a second, and appeared embarrassed. "Well, you may not consider it suitable, but let me show what is available."

Dr. Ahmed drove Mother Teresa and Sister Agnes through the narrow, crowded streets. Ahead loomed a tall conical temple. As the car drew closer, the doctor asked "Do you recognize this place, Mother?"

"Isn't that Kalighat, the Hindu Temple?" she responded. It was.

Kali was the Hindu goddess of death. Every year throngs of pilgrims came to pray before her tall, black statue. Kali's golden tongue hung to her chin. She was clothed with jewels. "Will Catholic sisters work this close to a pagan shrine?" wondered the doctor.

This Is the Place

The car stopped in front of a low white structure known as "The Dormashala." It had been used as a hostel by Hindu pilgrims.

"This is the place" he said, pointing to the building. "Naturally it will take a lot of cleaning before you can move in. Street gangs and criminals have been hiding out here."

Mother Teresa surprised the doctor. She beamed. It was just what she needed. The three stepped out of the car and inspected the place. There were two long rooms filled with trash and dirt. But each room had stone slabs on which pilgrims had slept. The slabs could be used as beds for the dying.

"Will this do?" asked the puzzled health official. "Because if you can use it, the place is yours."

Mother Teresa folded her hands together in the Indian fashion, and bowed. "Thank you, sir. We are more than pleased. We are very grateful."

Mother Teresa Takes Over

The next day a procession of Sisters in their white saris walked to the Dormashala. They carried brooms, mops, buckets and soap. As soon as the place was cleaned to Mother Teresa's satisfaction, she said, "Here is the new name of our home for dying destitutes. We shall call it Nirmal Hriday, The House of the Immaculate Heart of Mary."

Mother Teresa brought the first patients in herself.

They were poor beggars she found dying in the streets. No hospital would take them; no one else would stoop to touch their filthy bodies. They were caked with dirt, often lying in their own vomit and feces. Later the Sisters went out with litters to carry in people they found dying in the street. It didn't matter if they were Hindu, Muslim or Buddhist because Mother Teresa saw the face of Jesus in each sufferer. She offered them her total love and tenderness, teaching her Sisters to do the same.

The place became known as the Kalighat Home for the Dying Destitutes, where the poorest of the poor could die with dignity.

Complaints

Many nearby residents complained of the dreadful odor coming from the home because they feared diseased patients might start an epidemic. Some accused Mother Teresa of converting dying Hindus and Muslims. Neighbors threw sticks and dirt at the Sisters as they carried in their wretched patients. Local residents complained to Dr. Ahmed. In return he asked them, "Will your wives and mothers care for these sick people?" All shook their heads, "No." Touching low caste people was taboo. He concluded, "Then be glad the Sisters are willing to do it for us." That stopped the persecution for a while. Little by little the people of Calcutta came to appreciate Mother Teresa's dedicated work. They brought food, medicines and bandages. Mother Teresa never asked for financial help, but the city donated $20,000 a year toward her Home for the

Dying. She became known as the Mother of Bengal. Later she was called the Saint of Calcutta. Young women arrived from all over India asking admission to the Missionaries of Charity. Twenty-three Sisters had taken over the entire second floor of the Gomez house on Creek Lane. They slept side by side, crowded into the small space like sardines. A larger convent was desperately needed.

Mother Teresa began a novena petitioning heaven for a larger house. Each evening after work, she and the Sisters processed through the streets saying their rosaries, walking to Fatima Chapel. For nine days they petitioned the Virgin Mary to provide them with a bigger convent.

A wealthy Muslim had heard of the Order's work in the slums. He was impressed by the Sister's devoted care for the dying, no matter what their religion. When he learned of Mother Teresa's need for larger quarters, he offered her his house. He only asked that she pay for the land. The property consisted of three large buildings around an open courtyard. It was on Lower Circular Road, across from a trolley stop.

The rich Muslim told Mother Teresa, "I got my house from God and now I give it back to Him." After Archbishop Perier offered to pay for the land, there was nothing to stand in the Sisters' way. In 1953 they moved to their new home, and this became the Mother House of the community. Novices were trained there and professed Sisters went out to serve the poor.

Poorer Than the Poor

By then there were fifty Sisters, most of them Bengali girls. Mother Teresa insisted they live like the poor of India. They ate Indian food and wore the cheapest Indian saris. There was no running water in the Sisters' quarters. They filled buckets from a pump in the courtyard and carried them up the four flights of the building. One day a concerned visitor suggested Mother Teresa get fans for the Sisters. The temperature was almost 120 degrees. Mother Teresa replied, "Do the poor have fans?" Then she concluded, "Neither do we."

A wealthy industrialist asked Mother Teresa, "How is your work financed?" Again she had a ready answer, "Mr. Thomas, who sent you here?" Pointing to his heart, he replied, "I felt an urge inside." Mother Teresa settled the matter easily. "Other people, just like you, come here to see me and ask the same. When their hearts are moved by the Holy Spirit to help us, that is our budget." People of all faiths were moved to support Mother Teresa in her work. But no matter how many novices came, or how much money, food and clothing were donated, there could never be enough to help all the poor of Calcutta.

Calcutta was a city of seven million people. There were too many slums and not enough housing or jobs. There was too much disease. Thousands died of tuberculosis, cholera, leprosy and starvation. The hospitals and medical professionals did what they could. The city provided funds. Nothing could staunch the rising flood of misery of Calcutta's poor. Mother Teresa had taken on an impossible task. Yet she was never discouraged by the overwhelming misery and hopelessness. It was simply enough to help, by loving one suffering person at a time.

Leprosy

Mother Teresa's next big outreach was care of the lepers. It may seem strange that there were so many lepers in this century. We think of leprosy, now called Hansen's Disease, as a disease particular to Bible times. There were strict rules governing lepers in the Old Testament. Lepers had no rights and no place in society. They were cast out of their homes and towns. Lepers even had to cover their faces and ring a bell to warn others they were coming. Lepers came to Jesus to be healed. But, as time went on, every culture continued to fear lepers who were regarded as highly contagious. St. Francis was concerned for people who had leprosy. He even had the courage to hold a leper in his arms.

As late as the nineteenth and early twentieth centuries, leprosy was still considered contagious. Therefore, lepers were sent to special colonies in isolated places. The only people who would care for them were dedicated doctors, sisters, and priests. Father Damien of Molokai cared for lepers over many years. Eventually he died of the disease. He was recently beatified for his courage and conviction. Today most people know that you cannot catch leprosy by breathing the same air, or by touching lepers. Only those who lived closely with a leper for years contracted the disease. But leprosy spreads more rapidly in hot, humid climates and unsanitary conditions. All of these were prevalent in Calcutta. There were 30,000 lepers in Calcutta when Mother Teresa began her heroic work among them. Just as in biblical times, these tragic victims of leprosy were outcasts. Often their faces were mutilated by the disease, giving them a fierce, lion-like appearance. Many times their fingers and noses had fallen off. Some had to push themselves along the ground as their feet had rotted away. Lepers in Calcutta had only one means of support, and that was begging. They lived in culverts and under bridges. At night they scavenged through garbage piles.

Not all lepers came from poor families. Sometimes an educated professional discovered a white spot on his skin. This signified the onset of leprosy. He would be forced to leave his job and family. Most people were terrified of contagion—but not courageous Mother Teresa.

Mother Teresa Helps the Lepers

One day in 1957, a man with leprosy knocked on the convent door. When Mother Teresa opened it, she almost fell back in horror. The man crawling across the threshold had no face. Most of it had been rotted away by leprosy. Mother Teresa hugged the poor leper and invited him in and fed him. It was then that Mother Teresa directed her efforts toward the care of lepers. She already knew from her medical studies that leprosy was curable. Of course, there was always a risk in living closely with lepers for an extended period of time, but they were people, too. Lepers were human beings whom Jesus had died for. She would love them, too.

Mother Teresa felt it was worth taking a chance, especially since her Sisters had been trained in proper hygienic practices. They would just have to be extra-careful while nursing lepers. Most people afflicted with Hansen's Disease kept to themselves. They were afraid of being rejected by hospitals. Mother Teresa decided to try a new approach. The Sisters would go to the lepers.

A colony of lepers camped out near Calcutta's railroad yards, and along the river. At first the Sisters walked to these sites carrying bandages and medicines to dress the lepers' sores and stumps. They brought food and loving care. Soon their mission to lepers came to the attention of the Calcutta Corporation.

Help on Wheels

A mobile dispensary was donated to Mother Teresa for her care of the poor outcasts. Pharmacies donated drugs and bandages. Hundreds of lepers visited the mobile clinic and were given shots to retard their disease. Some even recovered. But Mother Teresa wanted a permanent place where these poor and despised sufferers could live in clean, decent surroundings. However she needed money, a lot of money, to make her dream come true.

The Indian government was grateful for all that Mother Teresa was doing, and in appreciation the Prime Minister donated sixty-four acres at Shantinagar, two hundred miles from Calcutta, for her lepers. There were no buildings, not even tents on the grounds. Lepers could not live there without shelter, but Mother Teresa's prayers continued to make her strong enough to continue to seek answers.

An Unusual Gift

Then the unexpected happened. Mother Teresa came into possession of a huge Lincoln Continental. Vowed to poverty, she and her Sisters had no use for such a luxury but the car could be turned into cash!

The long white limousine had been presented to Pope Paul VI during his visit to Bombay for the 1964 Eucharistic Congress. When he left India, the Pope turned it over to Mother Teresa. Mother Teresa had a brilliant idea. She would raffle off the car! Imagine her glee when that car brought in $100,000! Now she had the money to build housing for her lepers, and soon construction began at Shantinagar which she named The Place of Peace. There were cottages for families with leprosy, and dormitories for the sickest individuals. Those well enough to work raised pigs, vegetables and ducks on the land.

Shantinagar turned out to be such a great success that the Missionaries of Charity were invited to open similar facilities for lepers all over India.

Mother Teresa never worried about where to find money for her projects. "Money?" she would say. "I never give it a thought. It always comes. We do all our work for love of the Lord and He looks after us."

Although Christians in America aren't expected to take care of lepers, anyone of any age can donate money to help them. But there are many other unfortunates to help right here. Young people can express the love of Christ in their neighborhoods. They can visit lonely older people, or take flowers and cookies to a nursing home. Mother Teresa often said, "It is not how much you do, but how much love you put into it that counts."

CHAPTER FOUR

Spreading God's Love

Abandoned Babies

It wasn't long before God sent even more workers to Mother Teresa. At first three new sisters applied every year and then five a year applied, and by the time the Missionaries of Charity celebrated their 25th anniversary, the Silver Jubilee, they were five hundred Sisters strong. Mother Teresa couldn't do everything herself, nor could she be everywhere at once. She assigned seven or eight Sisters to each new house, placing one of the original ten Sisters in charge of the work. Sister Gertrude, one of the original nuns, was already trained as a doctor, and she instructed the other Sisters in care of the sick.

The numbers of the needy kept increasing. There were always too many poor, too many sick. With a population of 800 million, the Indian government was unable to care for all of them. Some of the poorest were beggars, but there were many workers who labored long, hard hours to earn just a few rupees a day. A few rupees were just enough to feed a small family; even one more baby would be too heavy a burden for very poor parents.

Mother Teresa Takes a Baby Home

One day Mother Teresa was walking through Moti Jeel on her way to the House for the Dying when she heard a faint wail. The nun stopped a moment to glance around and then saw where the cry had come from. A newborn infant lay naked on top of a refuse heap. Mother Teresa picked up the still-bloody baby and wrapped it in her white sari. At Kalighat she showed the abandoned infant to the other Sisters. "Look at this precious little girl. No one wants her. What shall we do with her?" she asked, cuddling the infant. The Sisters all cried out, "Keep her, Mother."

In Calcutta hundreds of unwanted babies were put out to die. This was so tragic to Mother Teresa that she needed to create another mission. "We must start an orphanage where we can care for these abandoned little ones" she said. And Mother Teresa promptly found a house to rent on Lower Circular Road near their convent. She assigned several Sisters to wash and feed the babies, and that is how Shishu Bhavan, a home for orphans, was started.

India was terribly over-populated, with unwanted babies left in garbage cans, on church steps, in convent doorways. One day a story appeared in the Calcutta newspapers saying that the Missionaries of Charity would take care of unwanted infants or children. Crippled or blind children that other charities refused were more than welcome. More and more arrived at the House of Orphans.

Finding More Babies

The Sisters even went to hospitals to ask for newborns abandoned by their mothers. Mother Teresa was happy to take these, too. The Sisters also helped unwed mothers, as the Catholic Church sought to promote Natural Family Planning. The Sisters opened clinics to teach unlettered women how to determine the days they were fertile, or unfertile. Some say the birth rate in Calcutta dropped, and as a result there were also fewer abandoned infants. Many babies were adopted by European couples who were unable to have children of their own. And many of these couples were happy to adopt a blind or crippled baby. One couple took in a baby girl with no arms or legs.

Up to that time all of Mother Teresa's work had been centered in Calcutta. The Archbishop had forbidden her to undertake work outside Calcutta during the first ten years of her Order. But as other cities in India learned of the loving care the Sisters gave to the dying, to lepers and to children, officials asked Mother Teresa to open similar clinics and homes in their provinces.

Spreading Out

When the ten years were up, Mother Teresa started work in New Delhi, India's capital. This was a modern, industrialized and banking city. There were many elegant hotels, palaces of wealthy Rajas and European entrepreneurs, and imposing granite buildings housing the various governmental departments. It was a city of sophisticated, educated leaders.

But there were also many pockets of terrible poverty. India's Cardinal Gracias invited Mother Teresa to work in Bombay and presented the Sisters a house in which to live. Soon vocations came from the wealthy young women of Bombay. Just as in the time of the first Christians, "Day by day God added to their numbers." Mother Teresa told the new novices, as well as the older professed Sisters, "This is how I would like you to be characterized: total surrender, cheerfulness, and trust in God." Her Sisters became known for their smiles and loving nature.

In 1964 Bombay was selected for the site of the World Eucharistic Conference. The Pope came, and television crews arrived from every quarter of the world to broadcast the colorful event. Millions lined the route of Pope Paul VI as he was driven through the city in an open car. The Holy Father visited the orphanages and clinics founded by Mother Teresa and was very impressed. He presented the little saint of Calcutta with the Pope John XXIII Peace Prize of $22,000. As was always typical of Mother Teresa, she put the money to good use right away.

A Famous Lady

This was such a prestigious award that Mother Teresa's fame grew. Photos and stories about her appeared in newspapers and magazines of every language. She was

photographed cradling a starving infant, washing the sores of a dying woman, or deep in prayer. Mother Teresa's plain wrinkled face became as well known as that of any movie star. The entire world admired her and her selfless work.

People everywhere wanted to honor Mother Teresa with awards, degrees and honors. But Mother Teresa hated giving speeches and drawing attention to herself. She said, "It is God's doing, not mine." But, in spite of her reticence, she often had to make speeches to raise funds for her constantly expanding charities. Air India presented her with a pass to fly on their airline, and eventually many airlines followed suit. If it were not for this generosity, Mother Teresa could not have traveled to all the cities presenting her with invitations.

Mother Teresa didn't just rely on contributions to support her work. She asked for the prayers of others to support her, and to give the Sisters the strength to work so hard. By 1980 there were 2,000 Sisters and Brothers in the Missionaries of Charity, operating in a hundred countries. None of this would have been possible without the prayer and assistance of the 40,000 co-workers. What are co-workers and when were they formed?

The Sick and Suffering Helpers

In 1948, Mother Teresa was preparing for her medical work at Holy Family Hospital in Patna. There, she met a Belgian woman, Jacqueline de Decker, who wanted to join Mother Teresa and work in her new Order. But Jacqueline was in very poor health with a spinal injury. After two years in the heat of India, doctors advised her to return to Belgium. Both women were disappointed at this turn of events, but the friendship did not end there.

In 1952, Mother Teresa wrote to Miss Decker: "I need workers, it is true. But I need souls like yours to pray and suffer for the work." Thus a support group was born that became known as "The Sick and Suffering Members of the Missionaries of Charity." Miss Decker was confined to bed with spinal problems. She had fifty operations on her back. Mother Teresa asked her to offer her suffering for the Order's work. Mother Teresa wrote further, "Why not become spiritually bound to our society? While we work among the poor, you share in the merit, the prayers and the work with your sufferings." Mother Teresa didn't push, but added, "Pray over this and let me know your desire."

Mother Teresa saw great value in suffering. It must not go to waste. She wanted the new Society of the Sick and Suffering to offer their pain for the work and for souls. Anyone was welcome, but members must live in total surrender to God, in loving trust and in cheerfulness. Soon about 800 joined the Society. Mother Teresa considered their help invaluable. One sufferer was assigned to each Sister to pray for her especially. Mother Teresa referred to Miss Decker as "my second-self."

The Co-Workers

Another friend was Ann Blaikie, an Englishwoman living in Calcutta. Mrs. Blaikie read in the *Calcutta*

News that Mother Teresa needed toys for a Christmas party at her orphanage. Ann Blaikie and many of her European friends met with Mother Teresa in early 1959. They assured the little Sister that they could collect enough toys for her needy little ones. They also gathered clothes and shoes.

Soon the group swelled with many members, some Indian, others European. Mother Teresa asked all of them to raise funds for her work among the lepers and they were happy to oblige.

Co-Workers Abroad

In 1960 Mrs. Blaikie returned to her homeland. Later that same year, Mother Teresa visited England. She appeared on television, speaking about her work in India among the lepers. A Mr. Southworth was already raising money for the Missionaries of Charity. Mother Teresa wrote, suggesting he meet Mrs. Blaikie, adding that she had helped with the work in India. These two, plus a few other English ladies who had lived in India, formed the first group of Co-Workers in England.

In 1965 Mother Teresa discovered that London had its own pockets of poverty and hopelessness. She asked the Co-Workers to help those in need in their own country. The idea grew and spread around the world. There are groups of Co-Workers of Mother Teresa in America, in Australia, in Europe and Africa. In 1969 the International Association of Co-Workers of Mother Teresa was formed, and their constitution was blessed by Pope Paul VI. Today there are 40,000 Co-Workers. They need not be Catholic; many are Hindu, Muslims, or members of a Protestant denomination.

What Co-Workers Do

Some Co-Workers meet every month for an hour of prayer together. Co-Workers are united by a newsletter mailed out three times yearly. Co-Workers don't just lend financial support. Many do small works of mercy in love for those less fortunate. They run soup kitchens, visit the sick, do laundry and clean house. They also do the shopping for those too weak or old to do it themselves. Some visit the elderly in nursing homes to do tasks such as shampooing and setting an older person's hair; perhaps they take them cookies, or just sit and hold hands with those who are lonely. Their mission is to offer love and smiles, and with these requirements anyone may be a Co-Worker, including young people.

Mother Teresa wrote in a letter to her Co-Workers, "Do you want to do something beautiful for God? Find a person who needs you. This is your chance to spread God's love wherever you go."

CHAPTER FIVE

AWARDS AND HONORS

The World Sees Mother Teresa's Work

By 1969 Mother Teresa's work was well known and admired all over India. That year something happened that brought her to the attention of the world.

Malcolm Muggeridge was a famous English author and journalist who no longer believed in God or organized religion. The British Broadcasting Corporation assigned him to produce a documentary about Mother Teresa. His heart was moved by this totally unselfish nun who was entirely motivated by love. Everything she did became "something beautiful for God," and consequently, Malcolm named his documentary, "Something Beautiful for God."

Muggeridge had lived in Calcutta during the 1930's when India was still a British colony. Amid the poverty of native Indians, he enjoyed the life of a well-off Englishman. He had servants, cool drinks and fine food, and socialized in elegant clubs and homes. No wonder he was unprepared for the heartbreaking misery of Calcutta of the 1960's when, following India's independence from England and its partition into two countries, Pakistan and India, millions were faced with war and starvation.

Trying to escape that horror, hordes of refugees poured into Calcutta, living and dying on the sidewalks and streets. Yet it was there that Muggeridge discovered Christ and Faith. His heart was touched by Mother Teresa, that one gleam of light in Calcutta. Her beautiful smile and burning love for the poor touched his hardened heart. He wanted to tell the world.

Accompanied by a top-notch crew of photographers, Muggeridge followed Mother Teresa on her Mission of Mercy. He attended Mass in the convent chapel and knelt beside her. The BBC crew spent five days recording the incredible work of Mother Teresa and her Sisters. They journeyed into the most wretched slums, they watched the sisters lovingly care for the sick and dying, they saw the homes for orphans, and, at the dispensary, lepers with missing fingers and toes. Then they recorded it for the world.

All Goes Well

The filming proceeded quickly and smoothly as though directed by angels. Expert cameramen were astonished when pictures of the dark Home for the Dying developed bright and clear. There were no hitches or blank film. In the designated time, Malcolm completed a 50-minute documentary.

Mother Teresa Becomes a Star

Television reaches everyone, everywhere. It enters the homes of rich and poor, young and old, believers and non-believers. Malcolm Muggeridge's beautiful documentary shook up a complacent world. The horrors of India's poverty shamed the spoiled and money-hungry millions of the affluent West. Here was something and someone totally different, someone they might never have known. The stark reality of Mother Teresa's work in Calcutta's slums brought her to the attention of the world and overnight the tiny nun became a celebrity. Funds poured in to help her work.

By the early 1970's Mother Teresa had established hospitals, orphanages and homes for lepers and the dying all over India. When asked how she found the funds to pay for it all, she replied, "Money? I never give it a thought. It always comes." Support came from big corporations, dioceses and churches, and even from the pennies of children who gave up candy and movies to help.

Large sums also arrived to cover the vast expense of caring for the world's needy. These were major awards and prizes that came to Mother Teresa throughout the 1970's. Perhaps this nun, vowed to poverty and humility, felt embarrassed by the huge sums and waves of publicity. But Jesus cried, "I thirst," to her each day from the crucifix in the convent chapel. And with these prizes she could quench the thirst and needs of more and more people. Each award included large gifts of money.

Mother Teresa never used any money for herself, only to quench the poor's desperate need. The money turned into new houses, new orphanages, new shelters for lepers and dying indigents. With each new honor that Mother Teresa would receive, she insisted, "I want the work known, not me. I am not important." She often referred to herself as "a pencil in God's hand."

But to others, she became a magnet. Protestants, Hindus, Muslims, reporters, heads of state, church leaders, all wanted to meet the "Saint of Calcutta" as she came to be known. Thousands of volunteers offered to work beside her in the slums. How did Mother Teresa accept these intrusions on her privacy? She made a deal with God. For every photograph taken of her for newspapers and TV, a soul must be released from Purgatory. (Purgatory is the place where souls must be cleansed of their sins before entering heaven.)

Nothing she did or said went unnoticed by the press, and soon the media made her a star. Mother Teresa's creased, weathered face was recognized everywhere. She was on the cover of *Time* and *Paris Match,* on the front pages of major newspapers. Even her name became a popular expression. A particularly good person was often referred to as a "Mother Teresa" type. With Mother Teresa receiving so much publicity, it was no surprise that she came to the notice of the Nobel Peace Prize search committee.

The Super Prize

One day in November, 1979, the sixty-nine year old nun was in the convent courtyard washing her sari in a tin bucket A young sister arrived with the news.

"Mother," she panted, "There is a man on the phone calling from Norway."

Taking her time, Mother wrung out the sari, dumped the water from the pail, and struggled to her feet. Fingering her rosary, she followed the young sister to the convent's only phone.

Mother Teresa greeted the caller with her traditional words, "Praise the Lord." Then a man's excited voice came over the receiver. She had won the 1979 Nobel Peace Prize! Mother Teresa's face showed no change— no excitement or pleasure. Honors meant nothing to her. But the poor, God's beloved sufferers, were always in her heart. Along with the gold medal came a huge cash prize!

Hesitating only a moment, the tiny nun spoke softly into the ancient wall phone: "Yes, I accept." Mother Teresa had not always been so ready to receive honors. The first time it happened in 1962, she was troubled. She had just been told she was the winner of the Padmashree Award. She asked Archbishop Dyer of Calcutta if her vows forbade her to accept an award.

"I suppose I should not go to Delhi to accept," she said to the archbishop softly. He answered her, "You must go. By this award, the President of India is honoring all religious who devote their lives to the poor." Mother went.

A Chain of Prizes

The Padmashree Award included 50,000 rupees. Next came the Magsaysay Award from the President of the Philippines, followed by the Pope John XXIII Peace Prize from Pope Paul VI in 1971. Also in 1971 she won the Good Samaritan Award in Boston and the John F. Kennedy Prize in New York. In 1972, Mother Teresa received the Templeton Prize from Prince Philip in London for Progress in Religion, and, that same year in Milan, the Ambrogino d'Oro Award. In 1975 she flew to New York where the United Nations awarded her the Albert Schweitzer Prize. (Schweitzer was a German Lutheran minister who was one of the world's greatest organists and theologians. He gave up everything to start a hospital in the Congo, first studying to become a doctor.) Each prize included large sums of money.

By the time she got the call about the Nobel Peace Prize, Mother Teresa was no stranger to awards and long flights across land and sea. As she had no possessions it took only minutes to pack.

Alfred Nobel

Who was Alfred Nobel, and why such enormous prizes? Alfred Nobel, a Swedish engineer, was born in 1833. He was the inventor of dynamite, as well as blasting gel which made it safer to use. Dynamite was originally designed to blow up rocks in mining and for the discovery of oil fields. Over the years Nobel amassed an enormous fortune. But shocked and saddened by the cruel uses of his invention in wars and the destruction of natural resources, he left the interest from his vast estate to fund annual awards.

These included prizes in literature, physics, chemistry, medicine, and economics, and the most prestigious was the Peace Prize. Nobel died in 1897. First presented in 1901, the Peace Prize was less than $100,000. By 1997 it had soared to over a million. In 1979, the little nun received $190,000.

In early December, the elite of the world flew in comfortable First Class seats to the presentation site in Oslo. Their name-brand suitcases were filled with glamorous clothes and jewelry, tailcoats and international decorations. But the winner of the award climbed the stairs to her plane in Bombay to a simple coach seat. In her wrinkled hand she clasped her only possession, her other habit, stuffed in a small cloth bag. Once seated, Mother Teresa immediately began to pray, fingering her wooden rosary.

Mother Teresa Arrives in Oslo

Oslo, the capital of Norway, was abuzz with the arrival of so many dignitaries, kings, presidents, ambassadors, and scholars. The tiny figure in sandals with her $2.00 cotton sari and threadbare coat might easily have gone unnoticed in such a glittering assemblage. But by then her rugged face was as well-known as the Pope's. Everyone was aware of who she was and what she had accomplished. Even the most important people strained for a glimpse of the tiny humanitarian.

On the big day of the presentation, Mother Teresa didn't have to spend hours at the hairdresser. Neither did she search through a packed closet for what to wear, or sit in front of a mirror applying make-up. It probably took one minute to put on her simple sari and brown sandals and walk out the door.

Mother Teresa didn't waste time. In Oslo she spent every free hour visiting local hospitals and charities. Then on December 10, 1979, the wealthy and famous crowded the Great Hall of the University of Oslo for the ceremony. A few friends and relatives of Mother Teresa were also invited. Among them were her brother Lazar Boxjaxhiu, and his daughter Agi, as well as the first two members of the Order, Sisters Gertrude and Agnes. Also included were co-workers Ann Blaikie from England and Jacqueline de Decker from Belgium.

Mother Teresa Receives the Nobel Peace Prize

In the great hall where chandeliers glittered and the celebrities watched, the bent figure of the Albanian nun stepped up to the podium to receive the world's most prestigious prize. John Sanness, Chairman of the Nobel Prize committee, handed her the certificate and medal. Robert S. McNamara, an American, a Presbyterian, and president of the World Bank, gave the presentation address. He said, "Mother Teresa deserves Nobel's Peace Prize because she promotes peace in the most fundamental manner by her confirmation of the inviolability of the human spirit. She does this by serving the poor, no matter what their race, religion, or political beliefs."

Seated on gold and velvet chairs nearby were King Olav V, of Norway, and Crown Prince Harold, accompanied by the Crown Princess Sonja. The award consisted of a large gold medal in a leather box, a certificate, and $190,000. Mother Teresa would use the money to open a new home for lepers.

Dozens of cameras clicked and flashed as reporters scribbled on their writing pads, observing every movement of the nun who cared nothing for fame. Later, when a reception was held for the one thousand dignitaries and tempting, tasty refreshments and champagne were passed among them by butlers, Mother Teresa refused anything, even a glass of water. The poor never had such luxuries and neither would she.

It was customary for the king to hold a banquet in honor of the new Nobel Laureate. Mother Teresa asked that it be canceled and the money ($6,000) given to the poor. Following the presentation, no one could find the valuable gold medal Mother Teresa had just received. The footmen and butlers were searching for it frantically when Mother Teresa arrived at the cloakroom to pick up her threadbare, second-hand coat. Her medal was found under the pile of ermine and mink coats of the other guests!

More Festivities

That night thousands of Mother Teresa's admirers snaked in a torchlight parade through the streets of Oslo. In the frigid December night, wisps of frost rose from their elated faces as they marched toward the Norwegian Missionary Society, where the nun from India was staying. Groups of costumed children met Mother

Teresa inside the warm building. They presented her with flowers and a gift of cash for her poor. They had sacrificed to raise it by giving up candy and movies, and doing chores.

On the following day, it was Mother Teresa's turn to give the customary Nobel Peace Lecture. Just as at the Prize ceremony, reporters and photographers pushed and shoved to get close to the "Living Saint." They asked personal questions and snapped pictures. The flashing lights bothered Mother Teresa's eyes, but she continued smiling. She always found it in her heart to love anyone. When the ceremonies were over, Mother Teresa left for Rome. She visited Pope Paul VI, and descended into the famed catacombs where early Christians hid out to worship. Many early martyrs were buried in those walls. At last Mother Teresa was free to return to Calcutta and her work for the poor. But no end of honors continued to pour on her once she was a Nobel Laureate. First the President of India presented Mother Teresa with the Jewel of India, the Nation's highest honor (she had already taken Indian citizenship). Once again Mother Teresa was off on another trip, this time to Delhi. She accepted the award in the Presidential Palace, the first naturalized citizen ever to receive it.

A Special Birthday

In 1980 Mother Teresa turned seventy. She had worked unceasingly among the diseased and poor for most of her years. Her large, comforting hands were gnarled and wrinkled from washing her own clothes, scrubbing floors, and cleaning the sores of lepers and the dying. Her back was curved from hours of bending over the sick, who lay on mats on the floor. In every face she saw Jesus. Every day she worked to fulfill the words above the crucifix in her chapel, "I thirst."

No work was too revolting or too demeaning for this woman who grew up in a well-to-do family. As Mother Teresa explained, "Without Jesus, our lives would be meaningless. We do it all for Jesus." For her birthday, India honored Mother Teresa by printing her well-known face on a series of stamps.

In 1981 an even larger cash prize presented itself. It was the Balzar International Prize, given only to those who promoted peace and brotherhood among all people of the world. The prize came with a check for $325,000.

A Woman of Conviction

Mother Teresa was firm as a rock in her beliefs. She also had the courage to stand up for them. She was invited to present the 1982 graduation address at Harvard University. At the outdoor ceremony, Mother Teresa's tiny form in its white sari stood out dramatically among the learned men and women in their black gowns and academic hoods. Facing her sat rows and rows of the rich and successful, anxious to hear the words of this famous woman. They didn't get what they expected!

On this occasion Mother Teresa displayed a sterner side of her usually gentle nature. Her eyes pierced them in reproach as she spoke out against abortion. "If a mother can kill her own child," she argued, "then what is left of the West to be destroyed?"

Her modern, humanist audience grew rigid with shock. This was not about the poor in India. Mother Teresa was directing her criticism at wealthy Americans. "What is more important to you: cars, televisions, the latest fashions? Why are you willing to destroy human life created by God in His image in order to enjoy more of the world's goods, and enjoy freedom from responsibilities of family life?"

This was nothing new; it had been a recurring theme in Mother Teresa's speeches worldwide. She was a staunch supporter of her Church's teaching on family planning, "Every child has been created for greater things, to love and be loved in the image of God." The Holy Father taught against the use of artificial birth control and abortion. American Catholics rarely observed this precept. However, Mother Teresa and her sisters instructed tens of thousands of Indian women to use Natural Family Planning. Mother Teresa spoke out in the same vein when she was invited to the White House by President and Mrs. Bill Clinton. As always, she was stalwart in presenting a most unpopular subject before a Democratic president who supported birth control and abortion as the normal rights of women.

Mother Teresa was a staunch defender of the Christian family and a good home life. She told many groups, "Love begins in the home. Go back to your family, your home, your neighborhood, your town. The home is each person's first field of loving devotion and service."

How can you make your home a place of peace and

love? Ask God in prayer to show you. Show love in everything you do and you will have taken the first step. The more places Mother Teresa spoke, the more famous she became. Her smiling, wrinkled face regularly appeared on magazine covers and the front pages of leading newspapers worldwide. She was on every list of the ten most admired women. But according to those who knew her best, Mother Teresa did not know what vanity was. Her focus was never on herself, but on others. No achievement ever stopped her overwhelming desire to help others.

CHAPTER SIX

THE FLYING NUN

Free Tickets

It used to take missionaries many months to reach
their stations in the heart of Africa or China. They
went by boat, train and on foot. Mother Teresa's trips
were mostly by plane. Vowed to poverty, where did she
get the money for such expensive flights? Well, Mother
Teresa was one of the most traveled women on earth,
and because of all the good Mother Teresa had done
for her adopted country, Air India granted her free
flights to anywhere it flew. Later other international
airlines did the same. Eventually, the Indian Government provided her with a diplomatic passport that
made entry into foreign countries easier. In the early
years, Mother Teresa expanded into other areas of
India with its 800 million people. Its cities' wretched
slums were filled with sick and starving refugees and
calls for help were many. How did she decide whom to
help and where to go?

63

Mother Teresa and her Missionaries of Charity went only where they were invited. Once the necessary funds and property became available, she made the decision to accept the call. Mother Teresa said, "We do our work for Jesus. If He doesn't provide us with the means, then He doesn't want the work done."

Off to South America

Venezuela was the first country outside India to request assistance from the Missionaries of Charity. It lies in the northern part of South America on the Caribbean Sea.

In July 1965, the Bishop of Caracas, the capital of Venezuela, invited the Sisters to work there. Sister Dorothy accompanied Mother Teresa on the long flight across three continents and two oceans to look over the situation.

The Bishop and local authorities greeted the Sisters in Caracas. They offered financial aid and help in finding them a place to live. Once the Sisters were settled and had opened an orphanage, Mother Teresa returned to India. She selected four Sisters to work in Venezuela. On the way there they stopped to see the Pope and receive his blessing.

A Great Need

Venezuela, as with most of South America, is considered a Catholic country, but it has few vocations and few priests. As a result the people know little about their religion. Still worse, many rural towns had no priest at all. As in India, the Missionaries of Charity worked in the slums, living much the same as those they served. Cocorote was the site of their first house. They administered Baptism, gave instruction in the Faith and prepared the young for Confirmation. They also carried Communion to the ill and dying. Soon two more houses were opened in Venezuela in rural areas.

Later, Mother Teresa was called to open houses in other South American countries: Peru, Colombia, Bolivia and Brazil. But the growth in South America never reached that of India. There the people were more responsive to Mother Teresa's charisma. But the need was equally great. Back and forth Mother Teresa flew across oceans to the Mother House, and her young postulants and novices.

Coming Home

Each time she arrived at the house on 54A Lower Circular Road, Mother Teresa was greeted with kisses and hugs. She blessed the eager young faces, holding them between her strong loving hands. "Mother," cried dozens of happy voices as the Sisters ran to greet her with "Welcome home!" Young nuns hung over the balcony, waving and calling her name.

But Mother Teresa was never home long. In 1968, Pope Paul VI called her to Rome. This ancient city is known for its great palaces, historic monuments and the Vatican. But Rome also has hidden pockets of slums as miserable as any in India. At that time there was an epidemic of drug use in Rome. There were many addicts, and later many victims of AIDS.

Also, for years, Italy had been under a communist government. Many Italians no longer attended Mass or received the Sacraments. Mother Teresa was delighted that the Pope had asked her to come to the Eternal City. Her Sisters would be walking on holy ground where the early Saints had died for their faith. They would be in sight of St. Peter's Basillica and the Vatican, the very heart of their Catholic faith.

As always, the Sisters lived among the poor in Rome's crowded slums. "Our Sisters go to the market and beg food for the poor. They teach the ragged children to pray and prepare them for the Sacraments," beamed a pleased Mother Teresa. Soon she established a novitiate in Rome. It would train young women from Europe and America who wanted to join the Missionaries of Charity.

Next Mother Teresa went in the opposite direction. She flew to Australia on the other side of the world.

Australia Calls

Bishop Warren of Broken Hill wanted Mother Teresa to come to Australia and work among the Aborigines. She arrived there in April, 1969. The Aborigines were the poorest residents of a country where everyone else was rich. Australia's natives were almost as backward as people from the Stone Age. They were small, dark people with wild black hair. Food gatherers, they lived far from cities in what is called the bush. As Australia's cities grew and expanded, the aborigines were pushed further and further into arid areas where they could find nothing to eat. Eventually many lived in wretched filth and poverty on the edges of Australia's inland cities.

A man named Mr. McGee asked to meet Mother Teresa. Once they were face to face he pushed a brief-case full of dollars across the table to her, saying, "This is to start." A few months later, Mother Teresa sent five Sisters to Australia to begin work there. They flew from Madras, India, to Melbourne, Australia. Their first day in Melbourne, Mother Teresa found a simple house in which they could live.

The Sisters scrubbed the floors and walls until the place gleamed. When they were done, Sister Monica, the Superior there, told them, "Go out to the streets and find some needy people whom we can help." The four other Sisters left in their white saris, anxious to get started. Up and down the streets they walked, but everyone looked well-dressed and well-fed. The disappointed nuns returned and reported, "There are no poor people here!" Sister Dolores came up with another idea. "Knock on doors and ask if there's anyone at home who is lonely or in need." The Sisters found people to help and the residents soon got used to their strange Indian dress. Eventually they discovered the work that they had come for. Many of the Aborigines had turned to liquor and drugs.

In 1972 the five Sisters bought land and built a Home for the Rehabilitation of Alcoholics and Drug Addicts. Once again Mother Teresa flew back to Australia to address the Eucharistic Congress held in Melbourne. She spoke of her mission to serve Christ in the poor.

"We must all see the suffering Christ in His brethren in pain," she told the delegates. She was very proud of what the Sisters had accomplished.

A Muslim Country

Mother Teresa's next big venture took her to the Middle East. Most of the people there are Muslims, followers of Mohammed. Islamic people believe they will go straight to heaven if they kill an unbeliever, and, to them, Christians like Mother Teresa and her Sisters were unbelievers. It could be very dangerous for nuns to live in such a place. Many religious Orders were forced to give up their work in the Middle East.

Although she was so tiny, Mother Teresa had the courage of a lion. She also had total faith that God would protect her and her Sisters. First, they studied Arabic, the language of most people in the Middle East. Then the Sisters went to work in Jordan and Israel. The Gaza Strip is one of the most dangerous places in Israel; fighting between Jews and Palestinians goes on year after year. In Gaza thousands of Palestinian refugees were crowded into camps surrounded by barbed wire. Few Americans or Europeans cared about their plight. But in March, 1973, during the worst part of the Israeli War, Mother Teresa sent her Missionaries of Charity to help the women and children in the camps.

Back in the Mother House in Calcutta, one day Mother Teresa told Father Edward Le Joly, her friend and priest, "Father, we are going to Yemen. We have been invited by the Prime Minister. He even presented me with a sword of honor!"

Father Le Joly's face broke into a grin. "What! A sword for a woman of peace!" "And Father," smiled Mother Teresa, "he has even promised to hold himself personally responsible for our safety."

Father Le Joly looked suspicious. He knew that few Europeans had been to Yemen, a totally Islamic country. Its towns were filled with minarets but there was not a steeple anywhere. Catholic Mass had not been said there since the last Crusaders left. Women in Yemen were clothed in black burkas from head to foot, and they saw their world through tiny slits in the cloth. In Yemen women had no rights and were not allowed to attend universities or drive cars. Father Le Joly wondered how the Sisters would be treated.

The Sisters Experience No Harm

But during two years in Yemen they experienced no casualties or insults. The officials built the Sisters a house to live in, including a chapel. The Sisters started a home for 120 unwanted children and also cared for adults with diseases and birth defects. Sister Gertrude, a medical doctor, set up a dispensary where she treated 60 patients a day. Once a week she drove to a leper village. The first time the Sisters went, the lepers ran away when they saw them coming. There was so much filth and garbage piled up that the Sisters couldn't get near the village.

Gradually, after many visits, the lepers lost their fear.

Then the Sisters got the government to clear away the rubbish and build houses. Sister Gertrude taught the lepers about cleanliness and gave them the latest medical treatment. The other Sisters helped the people plant gardens. They showed them how to make crafts to sell for extra money so that they could take pride in supporting themselves instead of begging.

Many of the children already had leprosy, so the Sisters isolated the few children not yet infected by the disease. The children were soon singing and praising God. While in Yemen, the Sisters had gone without daily Mass. Here they were thrilled when three White Fathers came so that once again they could attend Mass every day.

Mother Teresa Goes to Africa

Parts of Africa have suffered severe droughts over the past several years. As many as a million people have died of starvation because nothing could be grown. There have also been several ugly wars incited by tribal hatreds in which innocent women and children have been murdered. Thousands of families were forced to leave their native land and trek hundreds of miles to safer areas. Many died on the way. Mother Teresa's heart went out to these African sufferers. She begged food and supplies from various governments and churches to help them.

She Meets an Emperor

In 1973, Mother Teresa hoped to start work in Ethiopia. The ancient Christian kingdom had been protected from

Muslim invasion by its high mountains. It had been an independent empire since the time of Solomon.

In 1973 Ethiopia was ruled by Emperor Haile Selassie. Mother Teresa pulled every string to get to see him. She wanted to explain in person the work her Sisters could do for his countrymen. Finally she flew to Addis Ababa, the capital, and eventually met the emperor's daughter. The daughter convinced Haile Selassie that he should talk to the nun from India, and to please his daughter, he agreed.

Soon after, Mother Teresa was led through the ornate palace. Wearing her plain cotton sari, she was ushered into the emperor's throne room. Haile Selassie was seated on a gold and velvet throne. Chained on each side were his two pet lions. Fearlessly, Mother Teresa approached the regal, dark-skinned ruler. She explained what she would do in his ancient country. "If you allow us to come here," she said, "our Sisters will give wholehearted free service to the poorest of your poor. We ask nothing from your government to support our work." Haile Selassie broke into a smile. "I have heard of the good work you do. Yes, your Sisters may come."

As usual, Mother Teresa had won the emperor's heart with her sincere and direct manner. The Sisters arrived soon afterward. They were still working in Addis Ababa when the emperor was deposed and a communist government took over. One communist official remarked, "Mother Teresa is not involved in politics; she works only for the good of the poor." Surprisingly, the Sisters were permitted to stay.

America the Richest Country?

Mother Teresa had spread her work into countries that Americans considered poor and backward. Most of the people that Mother Teresa helped looked at America as the land of hope and opportunity. When New York's Cardinal Cooke asked the Missionaries of Charity to come to his city, many people were shocked. New York was the financial hub of the world, home of bankers and millionaires. Why would they need Mother Teresa?

In 1971 Mother Teresa flew to New York to see for herself. She was driven uptown along posh "Fifth Avenue" into Harlem. Instantly she was in a different world. The streets were piled with uncollected garbage; burned out, windowless buildings stood on both sides of every street. "Is this really America?" she wondered. It looked too much like a battle zone.

Not finding a decent place to live, the first five Sisters moved into the Convent of the Handmaids of Mary on 124th Street. They stayed one year.

The Order's real work began after Mother Teresa found a wrecked building in the South Bronx owned by St. Rita's Church. In 1973, after the Archdiocese renovated the place, at 335 E. 145th Street, the Sisters moved in. What could five women in saris do to change the life of children growing up in that drug-ridden neighborhood? The South Bronx was even worse than Harlem.

Helping the Lonely

Mother Teresa had often remarked that loneliness was the leprosy of the West. There were many old people barely existing on small social security checks in the same violent neighborhood. They rarely left their tiny apartments. Outside lay a cruel, hazardous world. Young delinquents brutally attacked old women, grabbing their purses, and knocking them down. Several elderly people were attacked and murdered in their own apartments.

Mother Teresa saw the elderly as a needy group. She sent the Sisters to visit them and bring joy into their barren lives. Some they visited were too old and ill to shop or do housework, so the sisters cleaned up their apartments, did their washing, and scrubbed their floors. Some elderly were starving, too afraid to leave their apartments, so the sisters brought them food or shopped in nearby markets for them. Visits from the Missionaries of Charity were often the only spark of happiness in these elderly people's lives.

Near the convent stood St. Rita's Church built in 1900. There the Sisters started a summer day camp in the church's auditorium. Almost 200 children attended. The Sisters offered after-school recreation programs, played with the children, and taught them crafts, songs and prayers.

Many families in the South Bronx came from Puerto Rico and other Spanish-speaking countries. The Sisters took Spanish lessons at a nearby high school. They walked two by two through these dangerous neighborhoods, saying their rosaries as protection.

Washington, D.C.

Once the convent was established in New York, Mother Teresa looked into helping other pockets of poverty in America. One of the worst was in Washington, D.C. Although there are many well-to-do areas on the outskirts of the capital where foreign diplomats, senators and top-ranking government officials live, certain areas of Washington are very poor. Mother Teresa flew there to investigate and locate some place to help Washington's poorest of the poor.

While there she also visited Washington's National Shrine of the Immaculate Conception. Patrick Cardinal O'Boyle gave Mother Teresa a large check to start work in his area. With it she opened a house in Washington, then one in Chicago, and another in San Francisco. Finally one in Miami was selected and opened by Mother Teresa herself. By the 1970's she had started houses in 40 countries. By her death in 1997, there were over 600 houses in existence. Flying back and forth between the Mother House in Calcutta and her various homes worldwide, Mother Teresa spent months on planes accumulating several million personal miles. In every place, and on every flight, she touched the lives of those around her. Mother Teresa's custom was to fly ordinary coach, refusing the comfort and delicacies of First Class travel.

No First Class, Please

But that was not always possible, as Donna Leeming of Merritt Island, Florida, recounted. She was a flight attendant in 1980 when Mother Teresa flew First Class on a Pan Am flight from London to New York. Mother Teresa and another Sister were directed to the large, comfortable seats in First Class. Mother Teresa had just won the Noble Peace Prize and was immediately recognized and treated as a VIP.

The humble nun objected, saying, "I'm sorry, we can't stay in First Class; we requested two coach seats. It is against our vow of poverty to fly First Class." The captain was called to end the impasse. "I'm sorry, Mother," he said firmly, his face red with embarrassment, "All the coach seats are taken. There are no other seats." Mother Teresa bowed to the inevitable, and sank down by the window. Her tiny figure seemed lost in the big leather chair as she lapsed into prayer.

A Gift Exchange

Donna Leeming has been a flight attendant all her adult life. She admitted nothing thrilled her so much as what happened next on that flight. "It was right before Christmas, when Mother Teresa flew our Pan Am 747 to New York. I recognized her habit and face immediately. As I took care of my passengers, this thought kept entering my mind, 'What can I do to help Mother Teresa?'" Then Donna, a devout Catholic, went to her wallet. It contained a $20 bill. She wasn't sure what to do. Donna recalls, "I had traveled with famous passengers before. I had always tried not to intrude myself on them." But the urge to help was too great. Going to the First Class cabin, Donna leaned over and offered Mother Teresa the $20 bill. What happened next shocked Donna so much, she is still in awe. "That little woman, almost 70, got out of her seat and into the aisle and grabbed me! She told me how wonderful I was. She made me feel as if I'd given her more than anyone on earth had given before. Then she handed me a card. On it was a picture of Mother Teresa holding a baby, and in her own handwriting were the words, "God bless you. Mother Teresa, M.C."

Donna could hardly believe it. She began dancing in the aisle, showing the amazed passengers her treasured card. Then she told the other flight attendants. "What happened next was incredible," Donna said. "All the flight attendants emptied their purses, gathered all the money in a hat and brought it to Mother Teresa." The famous Nobel Prize winner handed each donor a picture, signing it herself."

Donna was the only Catholic among the flight attendants. But Mother Teresa had touched the hearts of each. That was how she affected people all over the world on land and even in the air!

We can bring joy to others with just a smile or a few kind words. Traveling gives us the chance to spread love to people outside of our usual circle of friends and neighbors. Mother Teresa's message when speaking at churches, convocations, and Eucharistic Congresses was this: "We are carriers of God's love; you can carry God's love, too."

CHAPTER SEVEN

WORKS OF LOVE ARE WORKS OF PEACE

Men Join the Order

By 1985, Mother Teresa had established her Missionaries of Charity in fifty countries. A lot of the work was even done by men who had joined her Order. No religious organization of women ever had a branch of men before. But in 1963, twelve men asked to be a part of the wonderful work Mother Teresa was doing in India. After much prayer and thought, Henry D'Sousa, Archbishop of Calcutta, blessed twelve young brothers and one priest as members of the new branch. It would be known as the Missionary Brothers of Charity. Shishu Bhavan, on Lower Circular Road near the Sisters' house, became their home. The new postulants began their studies and work among the poor.

Within twenty years there were 401 brothers representing twenty-five countries. They worked in fifty-one houses around the world. The brothers wore regular shirts and slacks. Their sole identification was a small cross over the heart. The brothers, including a handful of priests who also joined, work with men suffering from AIDS, alcoholism and leprosy.

At the Mother House

In her late seventies, Mother Teresa was more in demand than ever. She flew anyplace she was invited to start a new ministry. Reporters, authors and photographers demanded her time. But the famous nun was happiest when at the Mother House in Calcutta with her novices and Sisters.

There she could resume the religious life she had chosen. There she had time for hours of prayer. In Calcutta she was close to her favorite work, caring for abandoned babies, the sick and dying. At the house she could take time to shape and develop young women who came to learn her ways. Their best lesson was Mother Teresa's example.

She taught them daily in the chapel. Dozens of young faces looked expectantly to Mother Teresa for direction of their lives and souls. She often asked them, "How can you truly know the poor unless you live like them?" Many of the postulants, both Indian and Western, came from wealthy families. The life of poverty was very hard. For that reason, Mother Teresa conceived the idea of "come and see."

"Come and Sees"

In the fervor of conversion, or a seeming voice from God, many girls rush to give their lives in service to the Lord. But young women can easily be deceived. Mother Teresa required that girls wanting to join the Missionaries of Charity first spend six months working alongside the professed Sisters.

Called "Come and Sees," these women were sent to do the most repulsive and demeaning work as a way of testing their sincerity. Any who stayed became postulants. If accepted as novices, their hair was cut off in a solemn ceremony and they received white veils. On completing the novitiate, they were professed as full members of the Order and donned the famous blue-edged sari. This only happened after much testing of their humility, obedience and desire to serve the poor. Mother Teresa had to be certain of their vocation. These young souls were entrusted to her care. It was as important to her as her duty to the poor.

Mother Teresa never exhibited any signs or weakness or fatigue. She knelt upright on the hard floor throughout the long hours of prayer. At other times she was constantly in motion. She almost flew up and down the convent's four flights of stairs. A tiny whirlwind of a person, she was motivated by love to put the most into each day. In every difficulty, she was certain God would provide. Her faith was boundless.

The famous nun insisted on doing all that was required of the other Sisters. At an age when elderly women are knitting in a rocking chair, she scrubbed floors on her knees and washed her own clothes. Chapels in her convents have no pews or chairs. The Sisters sit on the floor for teaching and kneel upright for prayer. So did she.

Mother Teresa, the Executive

In every decision, Mother Teresa turned to God for guidance. She had countless decisions to make every day. Thousands of sisters depended on her.

Although she had no degree in business administration, Mother Teresa was a great executive. She ran a worldwide corporation consisting of 500 houses, staffed by 4,000 Sisters and 600 Brothers. Established in over 100 countries, the annual budget for this charitable work ran in the millions!

Mother Teresa's charisma and wiles could soften hearts of stone. She never lacked for funds. Mother Teresa had the ability to get things done. She was an expert in building permits, bank loans, diplomatic passports, and sewer systems, and she drew maximum use from publicity. As chief executive Mother Teresa never slept more than three hours a night. She took care of correspondence until long after midnight.

She Got What She Wanted

Mother Teresa almost always got what she wanted. She even bent the Pope to her will. She had already established several houses of the Missionaries of Charity in Rome. But Mother Teresa wanted one *inside* the Vatican.

Each time she met with Pope John Paul II, Mother Teresa asked if the house was ready yet. The Holy Father admired Mother Teresa very much. "How can I refuse?" he was heard to say. So he ordered a brand-new house built for her and the Sisters inside the Vatican's walls. They immediately opened a soup kitchen. The headquarters of the Catholic Church had always been associated with wealth and priceless treasures. Now lines of ragged children and beggars came each evening for a free meal. Pope John Paul II sometimes joined other volunteers in serving dinner to the poor.

The Rich Lady's Sari

Mother Teresa was also practical. One day, an Indian lady came to Mother Teresa for advice. The woman had felt guilty about her extravagance. "What shall I do, Mother?" she asked. "I buy a new sari every month for 500 rupees." Mother Teresa looked neither shocked or disapproving. Instead, she recommended the following: "This month why don't you buy a sari for 400 rupees, and give the other 100 to the poor." The lady agreed and left.

The next month she came again. This time Mother Teresa told her to buy a sari for 300 rupees, and donate the other 200 to the poor. The following month Mother Teresa recommended, "Get yourself a sari for 200 rupees, but give the 300 difference to the poor."

A month later the lady came again. But this time Mother Teresa's suggestion was different, "Buy yourself a sari for 100 rupees, and give the rest to the poor." Again the lady followed the nun's instruction. Then Mother Teresa said,

"Stop, that is far enough. Each month buy a nice sari for 100 rupees, and donate four hundred to the poor. You are the wife of an important man; it is necessary that you look well-dressed to honor your husband and 100 rupees will take care of that nicely."

Too Much for the Little Nun

With so much of the world's cares on her stooped shoulders, Mother Teresa's loving heart was bound to give out. It finally did. She had been warned by doctors and clergy to let others take over some of her executive duties. But as her friend, Father Le Joly, sighed, "Mother Teresa is possessive of every detail of her work." That perhaps was her downfall.

First Heart Attack

Mother Teresa, then seventy-nine, was in Calcutta the day of her first heart attack. She was admitted to Woodlands Hospital on September 5, 1989, with a viral infection. Three days later, she complained of chest pains and was moved to intensive care.

On the edge of pneumonia, Mother Teresa was given heavy doses of antibiotics to fight the fever. A pacemaker was implanted to steady her erratic heartbeat. Pope John Paul II sent her his special blessing by telegram while the entire world prayed. By September 20, the famous nun was free of pain and eager to get back to work. A specialist from the United States, Dr. George Lombardi, examined her in Calcutta. He shook his head and reported to an anxious world, "Her heart is old, and she's not young anymore. At least for the time being, Mother Teresa will have to change her lifestyle." The doctor kept her in the hospital for six weeks. Finally, when they released her on December 12, doctors gave her strict orders to rest. Sister Nirmala, one of Mother Teresa's closest advisors, issued a statement to the public, "We thank everyone who prayed for Mother Teresa during these crucial days." Smiling and waving, the famous patient returned to Lower Circular Road.

Back to Work

Everyone hoped the aged Nobel winner would rest on her laurels, but she immediately returned to her back-breaking schedule. Mountains of correspondence flooded her desk, waiting for answers. There were new missions to start, old ones to revisit. She was off and running. While in intensive care, a stream of visitors had interrupted Mother Teresa's recovery. More lined up at the Mother House hoping to see her. Somehow she survived the constant interruptions and began to recover her strength. When asked about her future, the 79-year-old answered, "I just take one day at a time. Yesterday is gone. Tomorrow has not arrived. We have only today to love and serve Jesus." Once again she arose at 4:30 A.M. to attend Mass with the other sisters.

Many people were concerned about the future of the Missionaries of Charity. Was there anyone, anywhere, equal to the task? What sister could follow in Mother Teresa's footsteps? But when asked for a solution, or a name, Mother Teresa insisted politely, "It is God's concern, not mine."

Mother Teresa Goes West

Mother Teresa had always recognized that there was just as much need for her help in the West as in the East. She now turned her time and effort in that direction. She opened more homes in America: Detroit, Los Angeles, Newark, and Atlanta. "You are starved for love in America," she scolded. "You have no time for each other." And she said: "Love starts in the family: family first, then your own neighborhood. But it is not always easy to love those right next door." She always emphasized, "Love must start with *one* individual."

Election and Birthday

The rule of the Missionaries of Charity required the election of a superior every six years. Mother Teresa had always won. In 1990, while still recovering, she tendered her resignation, but Mother Teresa was elected superior general anyway. When the ballots were counted, her name was on all but one. That one was her own. She graciously accepted the difficult position, even though she was eighty years old, way past retirement age.

Mother Teresa's eightieth birthday was celebrated around the world. The Pope sent his greetings, as did leaders of many nations and religions. The Sisters made it a joyful event at 54A Lower Circular Road.

But Mother never gave any indication of slowing down. Nothing fazed her, not even wars.

Mother Teresa Saves the Children

Beirut, a city in Lebanon, was once known as the Paris of the Mediterranean, but civil war racked it throughout the seventies and early eighties. Mother Teresa had opened a home for severely handicapped children in Beirut. Most of the children were completely helpless, unable to walk or feed themselves. One day the home came under bombardment. Officials said it was impossible to move the children out of the battle zone. Mother Teresa didn't agree. She told them, "All things are possible with God." Then she fearlessly carried the helpless little ones to ambulances, and whisked them off to a safer part of the city.

During the Gulf War in 1991, Mother Teresa appealed to President Bush, as well as Saddam Hussein, to stop the fighting. When American bombs destroyed large areas of Baghdad, she went there under fire to help wounded children.

Nothing Can Stop Her

Mother Teresa collapsed again in Mexico, where she was setting up an orphanage. But soon she was off on another errand of mercy—this time to far-off Beijing,

China. Even its communist, anti-religious government asked for her help!

Next she flew to San Francisco to open a hostel for victims of AIDS. The bishop located a beautiful, multi-storied house for Mother Teresa and her dedicated Sisters. But vowed to poverty, Mother Teresa ordered the central heat disconnected as well as the hot water. She had the springs and mattresses removed. The Sisters ripped up the soft wall-to-wall carpeting. Soon, their bare feet were whispering across the cold floors. Mother Teresa lived as simply as her Sisters. She slept on the floor in an open dormitory. She used cold water for bathing and personal laundry. Still more economies were required in her houses. She insisted on turning off lights in the chapel when no one was reading! "No money given for the poor should be wasted on electricity," she explained. "We use only what we need."

The Importance of Silence

But stern as she sounds, this Saint of Calcutta exuded love and joy in everything she did, even the most menial and selfless tasks. Simplicity and silence were her two central messages. When asked what was most important about silence she replied, "Silence is essential in a house of religion—the silence of humility, of charity, the silence of the eyes, of the ears, of the tongue. There is no life of prayer without silence."

Mother Teresa Speaks in Washington

Once again Mother Teresa flew to America. She had been invited to address the annual Prayer Breakfast in Washington, D.C. on February 3, 1994. She looked even tinier, sitting between two six-footers President Bill Clinton and Vice-President Al Gore. Mother Teresa told the audience how her sisters feed nine thousand people every day in Calcutta. The focal point of her speech was that the greatest destroyer of peace was abortion.

Neglected Children

"Love begins at home," she began in her usual soft measured phrases. "Children have lost their central place in the family. Children are lonely, very lonely. After school there is no one home to greet them." She concluded, "To hold families together, they must pray together." The dignitaries lowered their heads in embarrassment. Everyone in America was guilty. Children were no longer a national priority.

Somewhere along the line, policy makers had forgotten that children are America's future. Mother Teresa never forgot. She was on the side of children everywhere, the born and the unborn. On every occasion, she spoke out for children's needs as well as for the rights of the unborn. At the conclusion of the speech, Mother Teresa expressed her disappointment that she was unable to be in Calcutta all the time to tend the sick. "One of the most demanding things for me," she told the assembled dignitaries, "is traveling everywhere, and with constant publicity." Discussions with Bill and Hillary Clinton at this same breakfast resulted in a home for infants and children in Chevy Chase, Maryland. It opened June 19, 1995.

Sick Again

The following year Mother Teresa was hospitalized several times with heart pains and an irregular beat. After experiencing difficulty in breathing, she spent her 86th birthday in a Calcutta hospital. The intensive care unit of Woodlands Nursing Home was filled with roses and birthday greetings. A banner outside the hospital read, "Happy Birthday, Mother Teresa! Long Life!"

Dr. Sik Sen, Woodlands Medical Director, declared the living saint significantly better. He allowed her to sit up in a chair to look over her many birthday cards. But a much more serious health problem arose in November, 1996. Mother Teresa was admitted to the same hospital with acute ventricular heart failure. A week later she was removed in critical condition to the B.M. Birla Heart Research Center.

Mother Teresa Has Surgery

Six heart specialists decided the frail nun required an angiogram. This medical procedure is used to locate blockages in the main arteries of the heart. Because of Mother Teresa's poor condition, the doctors were concerned about doing such an invasive test. When it was performed, the cardiologists discovered several dangerous blockages. Dr. Patricia Aubanel, who had flown in from Los Angeles, did the tricky balloon angioplasty. She inserted a thin tube through Mother Teresa's groin and snaked it up toward the patient's heart. The doctors then inflated a small balloon which pushed open the blocked artery.

Not far away at the Mother House, a hundred Sisters and half a hundred Co-Workers crowded into the chapel to pray for their saintly leader. It worked. A few days later, Mother Teresa sat up to enjoy chicken soup and crackers. The surgery had saved her life. As usual, though still weak, Mother Teresa was anxious to get back to work.

Another Setback

Sisters from her many houses poured into Mother Teresa's hospital room. With those who were her closest advisors, she discussed how to run the many, many centers of the worldwide Missionaries of Charity. No date had been set for her discharge.

Mother Teresa was still in the hospital in December when she came down with pneumonia. It was a terrible setback for her and the leaderless order. By then the Missionaries of Charity had 169 centers in India, as well as 517 in other countries. The 4,000 Missionary Sisters prayed earnestly for their stricken founder.

Following a series of antibiotics and forced rest, Mother Teresa began to recover. Shortly before Christmas, a pale and shrunken Mother Teresa was wheeled out of the hospital. She had been in critical condition for a month. Assistants supported the frail patient, many hands helped her into the car that took her home to Lower Circular Road.

A Slight Improvement

"Mother is coping well," announced Dr. Aubandel, when visiting her at the Mother House a few hours later. The happy Sisters greeted their long-absent Mother with cheers and hugs. "We are happy to have Mother back," exclaimed Sister Frederick, giving the Superior a hug.

Children at a shelter for unwanted children, prayed for their founder's recovery. So did millions around the world. But no one could hold her down. Mother Teresa was adamant about getting back to work. To prove she was ready, Mother Teresa laughingly demonstrated it to her heart specialist. "See, Doctor, I am so strong now, I can box with you." She held up her thin arms and jabbed playfully at the air.

Christmas Eve

But it was not true. When Christmas Eve came around, Mother Teresa was too weak to stay up for a Midnight Mass. The priest moved the traditional service back a few hours to eight o'clock. Mother Teresa sat in a wheelchair, singing hymns and carols along with the 300 sisters. The chapel had been decorated and everyone was smiling. It was the wonderful birthday of their Savior.

The next morning, Mother Teresa rallied enough to give a Christmas message. "Love, peace, joy and unity are the gifts of Jesus at Christmas," she told the large gathering. "My prayer for you is that you make your family something beautiful for God." Then she added one of her favorite sayings: "The family that prays together stays together." Mother Teresa resumed her paperwork, and took a few steps everyday to gain strength. She was very anxious to get strong enough to attend the Order's annual meeting. In January Mother Teresa resigned as Superior General because of her weak condition. All of the Sisters were to gather at the Mother House to elect a new one. Six years had passed since the last election.

A New Superior Elected

On March 13, 1997, Mother Teresa announced to the press that a new Superior had been elected. The Sisters had taken eight weeks of balloting to arrive at the selection. The new Superior General was Sister Nirmala, a Catholic convert and lawyer originally from a high-caste Hindu family. Mother Teresa had admitted she was too ill to continue as Superior. But it wasn't long before she was flying again.

Visiting Jesus in Prisons

"Inasmuch as you did it for the least of my brothers, you did it for me." It was inevitable that Mother Teresa would visit prisoners. But who would have imagined her going to Sing Sing. Sing Sing is an old, grim prison on the Hudson River, north of New York City. It is also the home of New York's electric chair.

On one of her visits to the Order's house in the Bronx, Mother Teresa decided to go to Sing Sing. She wanted to pray with the men on Death Row. The little nun walked between the cells, while the caged men inside rubbed their eyes in disbelief. Could this be the famous Mother Teresa who had come from India to see them?

Mother Teresa told the men that Jesus loved them. She held their hands. She smiled at them. Some of the big men cried. No one had ever shown them love before. By the time she left, a new spirit had entered the dark prison. Men awaiting the electric chair were filled with hope. Mother Teresa was against the death penalty, just as she was against the killing of unborn infants. Both were treasures of Jesus. He died for them, too.

When Mother Teresa flew to San Francisco, she visited prisoners there. After she left, Missionary Brothers of Charity continued her prison ministry.

A Kindly Gesture

By the spring of 1996, Mother Teresa was back at work, making appearances and helping the less fortunate. That was when Teresa Smith, a photographer from Boca Raton, flew to Calcutta at her own expense. She had offered to work with Mother Teresa. Terry was amazed at Mother Teresa's renewed energy. In spite of suffering from a broken collar bone, Mother Teresa attended morning and evening chapel services.

Terry, a tall woman in her forties, explained, "My first day at the Mother House, I went to chapel with the Sisters." She continued, "My foot was in a cast, as I had broken it just before my flight to India and hated to cancel at the last minute. I was unable to sit on the cement floor with the others. Seeing my discomfort, Mother Teresa stood up, dragged the chapel's only chair toward me, and insisted I sit in it. How could I refuse? Then Mother Teresa returned to the tiny stool she had been using."

Later that day, Terry asked Mother Teresa to autograph a book she had brought for that purpose from Florida. It was "A Life for God" about the saintly nun, written by LaVonne Neff and published by Christian Living Press. When Mother Teresa finished writing her name in that book, she pointed a crooked index finger at Terry, and commanded, "You see Jesus in everyone." This of course was the basis of all her actions, her underlying philosophy in caring for the sick and dying.

Terry Smith recalls that moment. "I looked into Mother Teresa's eyes and knew I was in the presence of God. Chills fluttered down my back. I could feel the power of her touch like that of an electric jolt."

Every day for two weeks, Terry went to help the Sisters at the home for severly handicapped children. One little boy was terribly crippled, with shrunken, twisted limbs. Standing over his crib, one of the Sisters rubbed his chest and legs until the child relaxed. Soon he dropped off into painfree sleep.

When her visit ended, Terry returned to Florida. But

she would never forget the love and devotion she had seen at the homes run by the Missionaries of Charity. It was a love they had absorbed under the leadership and example of their founder, Mother Teresa.

Mother Teresa worked for her beloved poor almost to the end of her fruitful life. Never asking special attention because of her heart condition, she continued to give of her immense love and compassion until her last breath.

Death came suddenly on September 5, 1997. The Sisters had been preparing to celebrate the 51st anniversary of Mother's Inspiration Day. That was when on September 10, 1946, she received the "call within a call" to work for the poorest of the poor. Instead of a joyful celebration, the Sisters had to plan the sorrowful funeral of their famous leader.

As Mother Teresa repeated so often, "Take one day at a time. We have only today to love and serve Jesus." Like her and her Sisters, we must try to make the most of each day. We can give some of it to God in prayer and good works. But we can also put our heart into our studies and other activities. Never neglect duties at home and in your family. Remember, we have only today.

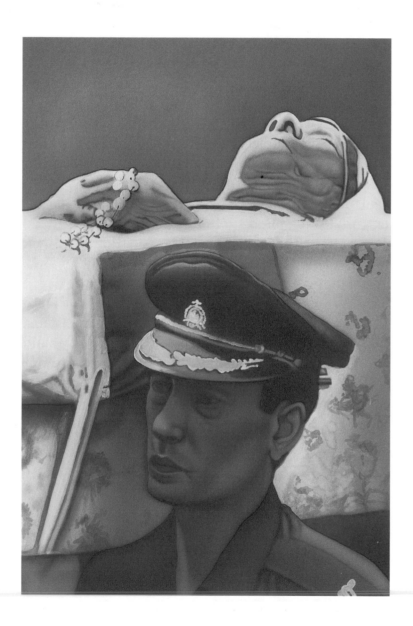

CHAPTER EIGHT

THE WORLD MOURNS A SAINT

The Last Day

On September 5, 1997, Mother Teresa woke up with a stomach infection. With her usual determination, the 87-year-old nun ignored her pain and attended morning Mass and prayers. As always, people were waiting to see her in her nearby office. With halting steps, Mother Teresa shuffled in to greet those who came for her advice and encouragement. To each she gave her blessing and a tiny religious medal or prayer card.

No one suspected this would be the famous founder's last day. As the hours passed Mother Teresa showed obvious signs of tiring. Sister Nirmala, new Superior of the Missionaries of Charity, tried to get her to rest. Fortunately, a leading heart specialist was staying at the convent in case of emergency.

Mother Teresa joined the Sisters for supper as usual. She then led them in evening prayers. Her weathered face looked drawn and gray. But no one noticed her worsening condition.

Mother Teresa's Final Words

Instead of working at her desk until midnight, Mother Teresa went straight to bed. Unable to get comfortable she called a friend to sit with her. Mother Teresa found it more and more difficult to get any air. "I can't breathe," she gasped. Those were her last words. Immediately the doctor was called to her room. As Mother Teresa struggled for air, he massaged her back. Then he tried to give the dying woman some water. The glass fell from her hands and shattered on the floor. Mother fell backward on the bed. The doctor attempted to revive her, placing an oxygen mask over her face.

Mother Teresa Dies

But it was too late. The greatest heart on earth gave out at 9:30 that night. Sister Nirmala broke the terrible news to the shocked Sisters. Within minutes she informed the media, and the world learned that Mother Teresa had died. The Indian government immediately made plans to give Mother Teresa a State Funeral. They wanted to honor their most illustrious citizen. Only two others in history had been given that privilege: Mahatma Gandhi, who won India's independence from Great Britain, and Jawaharlal Nehru, the nation's first prime minister.

The Viewing

However, it was the humble people of Calcutta, comprised of many sects and cultures, who felt the greatest pain at their loss. They wanted to see their little saint just one more time. To accommodate them, Mother Teresa's body was moved to St. Thomas's Church, where it was exhibited. It was in a glass enclosure all week. She lay in an open casket barefoot, and clothed in her community's blue-edged sari. Every day a hundred thousand men, women and children filed by for a last glimpse of their "saint of the gutters." She had sacrificed her entire life to relieve their pain and poverty. Parents lifted up their children for a better view. An old woman kissed the glass near Mother Teresa's bare feet. A bearded Sikh laid a rose beside the bier, already surrounded by floral wreaths. Rows of Sisters in the familiar blue-trimmed saris sat behind the coffin draped with the flag of India.

Funeral Plans

Meanwhile, world leaders of governments and churches prepared to make the long flight to India to attend Mother Teresa's funeral. It was scheduled for 9 A.M. on Saturday, September 13. The site chosen for the ceremony was Netaji Indoor Stadium, used for ping-pong and badminton matches. It could seat 14,000 safely from the monsoon rains of that season.

Sister Nirmala, elected the community's Superior General just six months earlier, now had the responsibility of making decisions about the funeral. But the shy, Indian-born nun, had known responsibility before. She had served as superior at many of her community's missions in different parts of the world. The 4,000 sisters scattered abroad now looked to her for guidance. Could she find the necessary funds and support to help the poor and needy served by their 500 clinics, missions and houses?

Sister Nirmala Speaks

At the funeral, Sister Nirmala told the vast crowd of dignitaries, nuns, priests, and Indian mourners, "The Missionaries of Charity are dependent on Divine Providence. God will provide whatever we need." Henry D'Sousa the Archbishop of Calcutta, echoed her words in his eulogy: "God is using the Sisters, and as long as they hold this conviction, all will be right, and all will prosper."

The week before Mother Teresa's funeral, Sisters practiced hymns, soldiers marched the proposed route of the hearse, and giant posters and photos of Mother Teresa appeared on buildings and streets.

In Washington, D.C. Hillary Clinton, just back from the funeral of Princess Diana in London, packed for the heat of Calcutta. She would represent the United States in place of her husband. Pope John Paul II appointed the Vatican's Secretary of State, Cardinal Angelo Sodano, as his representative.

The Procession

The day of the funeral, September 13, was declared a national day of mourning. Businesses, stores and schools were closed. Regular TV programming was pre-empted by solemn music.

The original route of the funeral procession was extended so more of Calcutta's mourners could watch. Mother Teresa's coffin was left open so everyone could see her. The bier was laid on top of a motorized gun carriage. Indian soldiers and red-turbaned Gurkhas walked on either side.

Behind it rode nine of Mother Teresa's original Sisters from the 1950s when she started the community, plus brothers of her Missionary Order. In another vehicle rode her niece, Agi Bojaxhiu, who had come from war-torn Macedonia.

The sad cortège rattled along the designated route. Hundreds ran alongside the bier, trying to touch Mother Teresa's body. Men, women and children of various ethnic and religious backgrounds leaned over bamboo barricades, calling out as she passed, "Goodbye, Mother." For Mother Teresa was the true Mother of all India. No mother could have held a child with more compassion and delight. No mother would have so fearlessly nursed a son dying of AIDS. No mother would have washed the stinking sores of a leper, as she did.

Jesus told his followers, "Love one another as I have loved you." That is what she did. "Inasmuch as you have done it to the least of these, you have done it unto me," said our Lord. That is whom she did it for, always urging her followers, "Do small things with great love." Mother Teresa set an example for all humanity to follow.

The Funeral Mass

As her cortège approached the indoor stadium, a band joined in. The Najida Stadium was packed to the ceiling with 14,000 mourners. The soldiers lifted Mother Teresa's open coffin gently off the gun carriage and carried it into the building. They set it down on a platform in front of the altar, raising her head so all might have a final view. On one side of the packed stadium sat about a thousand Sisters. Rising row after row, like a sea of white foam, many wiped away tears.

In front of the bier sat kings, queens, presidents and prime ministers representing forty-three nations. Assisted by an Indian soldier, each laid a floral wreath beside Mother Teresa's coffin.

First to lay his wreath was Sali Berisha, president of Albania, the country of Mother Teresa's family heritage. Next Mrs. Clinton solemnly put her red, white and blue floral tribute against the bier. The tributes continued until all representatives had finished. Outside thousands stood in the blistering heat for a final glimpse of India's saint. Inside guests from northern climates suffered in silence, fanning themselves with programs, wiping their glistening faces. The stadium's air-conditioning and fans were unable to cope with the large crowd.

Following the lengthy funeral Mass, leaders of various faiths gave eulogies, praising Mother Teresa. The first was given by a representative of the Archbishop of Canterbury. Others were presented by non-Christian leaders such as Sikhs, Parsees, Hindus and Muslims in their traditional robes and head coverings.

At the conclusion of the four-hour service, the Indian soldiers again lifted Mother Teresa's casket to their shoulders and slowly marched out. Billions of people worldwide watched the ceremony on television. It was replayed twice the next day.

Mother Teresa Is Laid to Rest

The now gray, decaying body was removed to the Mother House for burial. A cement crypt for her remains was quickly built in the former dining room of the building. Only sisters and clergy were allowed to watch as Mother Teresa was laid to rest. No press or TV cameras were present at her final event. The Sisters could mourn privately without thousands of sightseers clamoring to see where their benefactor had been laid.

Other Memorial Masses were celebrated for Mother Teresa in Rome, London, New York and Washington, D.C. at the National Shrine of the Immaculate Conception.

She Touched Everyone

The humble saint traveled everywhere, meeting with the great of our time: popes, kings, presidents, authors, stars of screen and stage. All basked in her presence, and no matter who they were they all felt the same way: "To meet her was to feel utterly humble." She also sparked a conviction in their hearts to give more to the needy, and to express love to those around them. Mother Teresa was gone, but not her message. Not her work. Particularly not her memory. The week of her funeral Mother Teresa's picture was in every major newspaper as well as on the cover of *Newsweek* and religious publications. Even the *National Enquirer,* a newspaper typically devoted to sensationalist types of news, gave her a cover story. The great question at the conclusion of every article always asks, "Will Mother Teresa be declared a Saint by the Catholic Church? How soon can she be canonized?"

Making a Saint

Constantly called a "living Saint," Mother Teresa would plead, "Let me die first." Now she was gone and her admirers clamored for instant canonization. Virtuous men and women are never proclaimed saints by the Catholic Church until after their deaths. Certainly the Congregation for the Causes of Saints will follow the rules. The formal process is not allowed to begin until five years after a candidate has died. In addition, medical and theological proof of two miracles obtained by intercession of the possible Saint must be verified. The process of canonization takes many years. However, due to popular demand, on February 28, 1999, His Holiness, Pope John Paul II waived the five-year requirement, allowing the process for Mother Teresa's "cause" to begin immediately. Now thousands of documents must be examined, and friends and fellow religious interrogated. Eight theologians and the Promoter of the Faith will judge the "cause." The essential parts of the procedure are three. First the investigators must establish a reputation for sanctity.

Mother Teresa certainly qualified there. The second is to establish the heroic quality of her virtues. Hers were beyond heroic. Third is the working of miracles, which must occur through her intercession, after her death. These will surely come.

Some Saints were canonized centuries after their death, such as Joan of Arc. Others, like St. Thérèse de Lisieux and St. Maximilian Kolbe, were canonized within decades. Mother Teresa has already been declared a saint by popular assent. No one doubts she will be canonized by the Catholic Church. It is only a question of time.

A Chain of Love

Mother Teresa was the most admired and inspiring woman of the 20th century. Her example of holiness, self-denial and good works was exemplary. She had the charisma to turn hearts from selfishness to selflessness.

Mother Teresa was God's gift to the world. She shone like a star in the midst of the darkness and ugliness of our time. Her love for all God's children, no matter their color or creed, broke down the walls that separate humankind. She made a difference in every life she touched. She said of her Sisters, "We shall weave a chain of love around the world." Anyone can be a part of that chain. We can all express love. We can reach out to those around us: in our families, neighborhoods, schools and jobs. It is never hard if you do it as Mother Teresa suggested: "One person at a time."

Mother Teresa is gone. But what she taught by her life

and words lives on. Be a pencil in God's hand and write a magnificent story. Do little things with great love. See Jesus in everyone you help. And even if you are but one link in the chain of love, know that "you, too, can change the world."

BIBLIOGRAPHY

Chawla, Navin. *Mother Teresa, The Authorized Biography*, Rockport, MA, Element Books, 1996

Egan, Eileen. *Such a Vision of the Street: Mother Teresa— The Spirit and the Work*, Garden City, Doubleday, 1985

Giff, Patricia Reilly. *Mother Teresa, Sister to the Poor*, New York, Viking, 1986

Gonzales-Balado, Jose L. *My Life for the Poor, Mother Teresa of Calcutta*, San Francisco, Harper and Row, 1985

Gray, Tony. *Champions of Peace, The Story of the Nobel Peace Prize*, London, Paddington Press, 1976

Lee, Betsy. *Caring for All God's Children*, Minneapolis, Dillon, 1981

Le Joly, Edward. *Mother Teresa of Calcutta*, Calcutta, St. Paul Publications 1983

Le Joly, Edward. *Mother Teresa: The Joy of Loving*, New York, Harper and Row, 1989

Le Joly, Edward. *Servant of Love: Mother Teresa and Her Missionaries of Charity*, New York, Harper and Row, 1977

McGovern, James. *To Give the Love of Christ*, New York, Paulist Press, 1978

Muggeridge, Malcolm. *Something Beautiful for God*, New York, Doubleday, 1971

Podojil, Catherine. *Mother Teresa,* Glenview, IL., Scott
Foresman, 1982
Vardey, Lucinda. *Mother Teresa, A Simple Path,* New York,
Ballantine Books, 1995
Magazine Articles in: *Time, Newsweek, Catholic Digest,
Reader's Digest, Parade*
Newspaper Articles in: *USA Today, Florida Today, Dallas
Morning News, Los Angeles Times, Sarasota Herald
Tribune, Orlando Sentinel*